THE
250
BEST
muffin
RECIPES

Esther Brody

THE
250
BEST
muffin

RECIPES

Esther Brody

Robert
ROSE

The 250 best muffin recipes

For complete cataloging information, see page 6.

DESIGN, EDITORIAL AND PRODUCTION:	MATTHEWS COMMUNICATIONS DESIGN INC.
PHOTOGRAPHY:	MARK T. SHAPIRO
ART DIRECTION, FOOD PHOTOGRAPHY:	SHARON MATTHEWS
FOOD STYLIST:	KATE BUSH
PROP STYLIST:	CHARLENE ERRICSON
MANAGING EDITOR:	PETER MATTHEWS
INDEX:	BARBARA SCHON
COLOR SCANS & FILM:	POINTONE GRAPHICS

We acknowledge the financial support of the Government of Canada through the Book Publishing Industry Development Program (BPIDP) for our publishing activities.

Canadä

Published by: Robert Rose Inc. • 156 Duncan Mill Road, Suite 12
Toronto, Ontario, Canada M3B 2N2 Tel: (416) 449-3535

Printed in Canada

234567 BP 02 01 00

contents

Canadian Cataloguing in Publication Data

Brody, Esther
  The 250 best muffin recipes

Includes index.
ISBN 0-7788-0014-8

1. Muffins.   I. Title.

TX770.M83B76 1999   641.8'15   C99-931250-2

dedication

To my daughter, Lisa Michelle
who spent countless hours in the wee morning helping
me bake and wrap muffins.

To my son, Leonard Jason
who also spent many hours carrying and delivering
trays of muffins with me.

In memory of my mother, Mary
who was a wonderful cook and whose talents I like to
think I have inherited, if only in part.

acknowledgements

To the many friends in many places who so willingly and graciously shared their family or special recipes with me, I want to express my thanks and deep appreciation.

And to the following people who encouraged and assisted me in so many ways:

The Ranchman's

Lynette and Harris Dvorkin

Bishop Morrow Insurance

Blue Flame Kitchen

Beryl Turner

Ellen Greenwood

Colleen Steinstra

Dr. Jane Parney

Arlene Kushner

Maria Buchwald

Sophie Mah

Shauna, David, Drew and Brandon Jackson

and my sisters Betty and Cecille

introduction

I REALLY DON'T REMEMBER how my muffin career began, but it was long before muffin specialty shops and franchises started appearing.

Muffins have always seemed healthier than danishes, doughnuts and even cinnamon buns — although I love all three. They are good to eat at any time of the day and can be made with a wide variety of healthy, nutritious ingredients such as bran, whole wheat, oats, and wheat germ — as well as not-so-healthy (but oh-so-good) things like chocolate.

Muffins are endlessly adaptable; you can vary their flavor and appearance by adding fruit (such as dates, raisins, blueberries, apples), chopped nuts or chocolate chips. You can use brown or white flour, sugar or syrup. Muffins can be sprinkled with various toppings, split in half and covered with favorite spreads and served warm or cold. They make wonderful additions to children's or adult's lunches. And they're always a welcome snack.

With a high fiber content, muffins can be a part of any well-balanced diet. Who says being healthy has to be dull?

Most muffin recipes can be put together from ingredients you usually have on hand and need to use up, such as overripe bananas or other perishable fruits such as strawberries, peaches or nectarines.

To some people, baking muffins sounds simple: just measure the ingredients, mix well and bake. Well, the procedure *is* simple — at least, once you've mastered the basic techniques and have learned how to avoid the pitfalls that can come along the way.

In this book, I have attempted to pull together everything that I have learned over the years — all the secret tips, general baking information, as well as all my favorite recipes so that you, too, can bake big, beautiful, moist and tasty muffins. To me, making "good" muffins is an art and if you master the correct techniques to proper muffin baking, you should have no problems.

This book is the direct result of all the positive feedback that my muffins have received over the years. In fact, I have lost track of the number of times that people have raved about my muffins' moistness, large uniform size and shape, and their flavor. So a few years ago, when a few deli and smoke shops asked me to supply them with my muffins, I decided to give it a try.

I recall once meeting a truck driver who said he didn't eat muffins anymore because they all seemed so dry, small and tasteless. So I gave him a complimentary bag of muffins to take on his drive back to British Columbia and was thrilled to receive a long distance call a few days later telling me how great they were and that he was a muffin fan again. His company and fellow workers wanted me to consider shipping muffins to them weekly, but I had to decline, since I was having enough trouble keeping up with demands in my own city!

Another incident I recall fondly occurred in a build-ing to which I delivered muffins daily, and where there was great demand for my rhubarb muffins. It was so great, in fact, that my small garden was soon unable to supply the fresh rhubarb required. Well, it wasn't long before the people in that building were bringing me bags of fresh rhubarb from their gardens; attached were notes asking me to keep making muffins!

At times, I had asked some of my distributors to specify which muffin varieties their customers like best, since I often didn't have time to make as many flavors as I'd like. But they always told me that their customers loved all the different flavors and were happy to buy whatever I brought in. It was a wonderful compliment, but very frustrating for me having to decide which of my hundreds of muffin recipes would please the greatest number of people. Still, it was great knowing people trusted me enough to supply what I felt was best.

Over the years, I have come to be known as "The Muffin Lady." In fact, to this day, some people still don't know my real name!

People have sent me their favorite recipes from all over, including the United States and Europe. Some have given me permission to use their names but others preferred I didn't, so I have decided to eliminate names completely. It also became a kind of hobby for me to collect recipes from newspapers and magazines, as well as restaurants I have been to that were kind enough to share their special recipes with me.

Some years ago, I began to realize that I just couldn't keep up with the demand all by myself. I had responsibilities as a single parent with a house to run and a full-time job. I eventually had to inform my customers that I was retiring. To this day, I still get calls from people asking me to supply them with muffins or to share my muffin recipes and secrets. So, I decided to write a book as a special thanks to all those people whose compliments I have cherished and who have provided me with so much encouragement.

There is no such thing, I believe, as an original muffin recipe. Good recipes are handed down in families, given over to friends, and people usually adapt recipes to suit their own particular tastes. Every time I have come upon a new recipe, I tried it out in one or two shops. If it was good, it went in my "yes" file, if not it was discarded. I wish now that I had kept notes on all these recipes so that I could have shared my thoughts and opinions with you. In some 20 years of muffin making I have obviously made so many kinds of muffins that it is hard to remember exactly what I liked about each one — and I never thought I'd be writing a cookbook!

Tired of the same old bran, blueberry and carrot muffins? Well, I think the variety of recipes in this book will awaken your interests again.

So pick a recipe — and bake away to your heart's content!

— *Esther Brody*

10 steps to perfect muffins

To achieve perfect baking results, just follow these basic steps:

1 Read the recipe carefully and check the required ingredients, oven temperature and baking time.

2 Remove shortening, butter or margarine from the refrigerator 1 hour before mixing. Unless the recipe states otherwise, take milk and eggs out of the refrigerator as you start mixing.

3 Adjust the oven racks to the desired level. I always bake muffins or cakes in the middle of the oven on the center rack.

4 Preheat oven thoroughly to the recommended temperature in your recipe. This is important for maximum rise as a too cool temperature will result in nearly flat muffins.

5 Collect all of the utensils that you will require.

6 Set out the remaining ingredients that you will require.

7 Prepare the muffin tins. You can grease them, spray them with vegetable spray or I prefer to line the tins with paper baking cups.

8 Check the recipe again for the method of baking to be used.

9 Spoon the batter into greased or paper-lined muffin tins, filling two-thirds to three-quarters full. Any cups not filled with batter should be filled halfway with water. This will not only save the muffin pans but will add moisture to the oven, enlarging the muffins and allowing for even baking.

10 Bake as your recipe directs. Muffins are done when they are golden brown, firm to the touch, come away from the sides of the pan and a toothpick inserted in the center comes out clean and dry.

muffin baking techniques

Successful muffin making depends on three important activities — measuring, mixing and baking. Let's look at each of these in turn.

Measuring

For best baking results, it is essential to measure ingredients accurately each time.

Have measuring cups for both dry and liquid ingredients ready — it saves time to have large measures also.

Make sure that your measuring spoons are in good shape, not warped, bent or dented, as you can't get perfect measurements if they are.

DRY INGREDIENTS

Use measuring cups with a flat rim so the ingredients can be easily leveled off.

Use aluminum or plastic sets that hold the exact amount needed when leveled off.

For less than 1/4 cup (50 mL) use your standard measuring spoons.

Fill standard measuring cups or spoons to over-flowing, then level off using a straight-edged knife or spatula — do not pack or bang on table.

FLOUR. We know that flour, no matter what type, is never sifted before it is measured. Any dry ingredients (like salt, baking powder or baking soda) should be sifted with the flour.

When a recipe calls for "sifted" flour, it should be sifted first and then measured.

If a recipe calls for "sifting the dry ingredients together," there is no need to sift the flour prior to measuring. Just sift all pre-measured dry ingredients together and proceed with the recipe.

You can use a scoop or spoon to add flour to the measuring cup. When it is full, level off any excess with the straight edge of a knife.

I find that the best way to measure flour is to choose a measure of the correct size with a flush rim for leveling. Fill it to over-flowing by dipping it into the package directly. Do not bang the measuring cup on the table, but level off with the straight edge of a knife or spatula.

Older cookbooks call for flour to be sifted before measuring but today most flours are pre-sifted.

BAKING POWDER AND BAKING SODA. Dip measuring spoon into container and level off with the edge of a knife.

To measure 1/8 tsp (0.5 mL), halve 1/4 tsp (1 mL) with the tip of a knife.

Dry ingredients such as baking soda, baking powder and cocoa sometimes have a tendency to pack down in their containers so before measuring, stir to loosen.

BROWN SUGAR. If a recipe calls for "firmly packed" brown sugar, spoon into a measuring cup, pack it down firmly with the back of a spoon and then level off.

LIQUID INGREDIENTS

Always use a see-through glass or plastic measure with volume amounts marked on the outside.

Place glass measuring cup on a flat surface. Bend down so that you can read the measure at eye level.

Make sure that your liquid measuring cup has a safety rim above the full cup mark in order to get an accurate measurement without spilling a drop.

OIL OR MELTED FAT. Dip measuring spoon into the oil and then lift out carefully. The spoon should be so full that it will not hold another drop.

SHORTENING. Partly fill a measuring cup with water, leaving space for the amount of shortening to be measured. Add shortening until the water moves up to the 1 cup (250 mL) mark or press the shortening firmly into the fractional cup so that no air holes are left. Level off and scoop out.

Mixing

A key factor in producing successful muffins is the mixing. Your muffins will be lighter when you mix them together quickly and lightly as this produces the best rising effect.

When a muffin batter is overmixed it is too smooth and flows readily leaving the spoon in a long ribbon-like strand.

This will result in tough muffins with funnels and a pronounced peak. Muffins should always be light and tender and baked to a golden brown. The secret for accomplishing this is not to overmix or stir. Use as few strokes as possible — the batter should look lumpy. I stir and mix my muffin batter with a "folding-in" movement using a large stainless steel spoon, not a spatula as you would normally when "folding" in a recipe.

In most of my muffin recipes I fill the muffin tins full, right to the top, unless I am adding a filling or topping, to produce large and even-sized muffins.

I prefer to use the standard method with most of my recipes, unless the recipe states otherwise. I find it the easiest way.

Dry ingredients should be thoroughly mixed in one bowl and liquid ingredients in another bowl. When separated like this they can be left indefinitely. But as soon as you combine the two of them, you have to work quickly, stirring just to enough to moisten and combine. Then spoon immediately into muffin tins.

The batter for muffins is usually stirred but may be creamed.

For a stirred batter, the dry ingredients are mixed together in order to evenly distribute the baking powder and baking soda. If the leavening is unevenly distributed, the muffins may have a bitter taste.

For a creamed batter, the shortening and sugar are beaten together before adding the other ingredients. The muffins are usually sweeter and have a cake-like texture.

Once the muffin batter has been prepared and put into the muffin tins it should go into the oven quickly. The idea is for the batter to start rising in the oven not on the counter. That is why I prepare the muffin tins before I start mixing the recipe and I have all of the ingredients ready, including any grating.

Baking

There are two common methods for baking muffins:

THE STANDARD METHOD

1. Sift the dry ingredients into a large bowl and make a well or depression in the center. Remember to mix dry ingredients together well in order to distribute the baking powder and baking soda evenly.

2. Combine the egg (slightly beaten), milk and oil or melted shortening (cool the melted butter or shortening first).

3. Add the liquid ingredients all at once to the dry ingredients.

4. Stir quickly only until the dry ingredients are moist. The batter will be slightly lumpy.

5. Spoon batter into prepared muffin tins, filling two-thirds full.

6. Bake as directed.

THE BISCUIT METHOD

1. Cut shortening into the sifted dry ingredients until crumbly.

2. Combine the egg and milk. Add all at once to the flour mixture.

3. Stir just until moist.

4. Spoon batter into prepared muffin tins, filling two-thirds full.

5. Bake as directed. Most muffin recipes suggest baking at 375° F (190° C) or 400° F (200° C). I have found that baking at 425° F (220° C) for 20 minutes works best for my muffins.

If the muffins brown too quickly turn your oven down.

Muffins bake best on the middle rack in the oven. On the lowest shelf the bottoms burn too quickly and on the highest shelf the tops brown too soon.

I set my timer for 15 minutes and then I turn the muffin pan around in the oven, putting front to back. Then I set the timer for 5 minutes and bake for the remaining 5 minutes.

Most ovens cook unevenly, but I have found that my method of turning for the last 5 minutes of baking produces a more evenly baked and browned muffin.

Check the accuracy of your oven often and make any necessary adjustments. It is quite normal for ovens to vary. Also, ovens often bake faster at the back, that is why I turn the muffin pan around for a more even baking.

Muffins straight from the hot oven are very fragile so allow the pan to cool for about 5 to 10 minutes before removing the muffins from the pan. The steam from the pan should loosen them. If they still stick, loosen the muffins by running a knife around the edge of the cup. Often you can simply turn the pan upside-down and the muffins will fall out.

If you are baking fruit-filled muffins, cool completely before removing them from the tins.

If you wish to keep muffins hot for serving, loosen them and tilt to one side of the muffin tin slightly. It is a good idea to place them in the warm, turned off oven until you are ready to serve.

general muffin tips

- Because muffins are great warm, you can reheat them by wrapping loosely in foil and placing in the oven at 400° F (200° C) for about 5 to 10 minutes. If frozen, heat for about 15 to 20 minutes.

- Muffins can be heated in the microwave by covering with a damp paper towel. Heat for about 30 seconds or just until warm. But be careful, microwaves heat very quickly.

- Muffins can be baked successfully in the microwave using special microwave muffin pans or glass custard cups. Be sure to follow the manufacturer's directions that come with your microwave oven for proper baking time and power levels. I don't use my microwave for baking very often because I get the best results from a regular oven, but I know people who get great results from their microwaves.

- The yield amount in most recipes is based on filling the muffin tins about two-thirds full. When filling tins to the top you will yield 2 or 3 less muffins.

- For smaller muffins, use medium-sized paper baking cups. The yield will be 3 or 4 muffins greater. You should reduce the baking time slightly, usually up to 5 minutes.

- Whether I plan on freezing the muffins or eating them in the next few days, I wrap each muffin separately in plastic wrap. Once wrapped, They have a terrific shelf life of 3 to 5 days. They will stay moist and fresh and ready to go.

- I do not store muffins in the refrigerator as they become stale and dry faster. Keep them on the counter or in the freezer.

- Muffins freeze well for up to 6 months or more if wrapped properly. To freeze muffins, cool completely first. Wrap in plastic and place on a foil or styrofoam tray. Place tray in a large airtight freezer bag and tie securely. This double wrap prevents the freezer taste you sometimes get when foods thaw.

- To heat frozen muffins, unwrap and thaw. Place

muffins in greased muffin tins and heat slowly at 300° F (150° C) or until just warm.

🧁 Instead of baking muffins immediately you can freeze them by spooning the batter into paper baking cups. Place cups in the freezer. When frozen, place the frozen cups into airtight containers or freezer bags and return to the freezer. To bake, unwrap and place the paper cups and frozen batter into ungreased muffin tins. Bake in a preheated oven 300° F (150° C) until well risen. Then increase oven temperature to 425° F (220° C) and finish baking for 15 to 20 minutes or until golden brown. If you wish to thaw the muffins first, it usually takes about 1 hour. Bake thawed muffins in preheated oven 425° F (220° C) for 15 to 20 minutes or until golden brown.

🧁 If you begin to find that seeing so many muffin recipes gets confusing, check for ingredients you know and like and then try that particular recipe.

muffin troubleshooting

If your muffins are less than perfect, here are some important tips:

Muffins are too hard.
There is too much flour and not enough liquid. Try using 1/4 cup (50 mL) less flour.

You may have stirred too long and hard. Try mixing for only 10 seconds.

Muffins are flat or spreading.
If they are spreading out all over the top of the tins, don't fill as full.

There could be too much liquid in the batter. Try using 1/4 cup (50 mL) less liquid.

Muffins are tough and soggy, peaks in center.
You have probably over-mixed which toughens the batter.

Underbaking could be causing the problem as ovens vary in temperatures. Try turning up your oven 25 degrees and shorten the baking time.

Muffins rise high, fall flat in center.
There is not enough flour. Increase the amount by about 1/4 cup (50 mL). Sometimes the eggs are so large that they increase the ratio of liquid ingredients. Use large eggs but not extra large.

Muffins do not brown.
If they do not brown easily, your oven rack is too high or too low.

If muffins are baked on the lowest rack, they may burn on the bottom before being done on top.

If muffins are baked on the highest rack, they will get too brown on top.

Always use the middle rack for an even browning.

Muffins are coarse-textured.
This is usually caused from insufficient stirring and baking at too low a temperature.

classic muffins

basic muffin

2 cups	all-purpose flour	500 mL
4 tsp	baking powder	20 mL
1/2 tsp	salt	2 mL
2 tbsp	granulated sugar	25 mL
1 cup	milk	250 mL
2	eggs, beaten	2
3 tbsp	melted butter or margarine or shortening	45 mL

Preheat oven to 400° F (200° C)
Muffin tin, lightly greased

1. In a large bowl sift together flour, baking powder, salt and sugar. Make a well in the center.

2. In another bowl, combine milk, beaten eggs and melted butter. Pour into dry ingredients. Mix just until blended, no more than 15 to 20 strokes. Do not overmix.

3. Spoon batter into prepared muffin tin, filling two-thirds full. Bake in preheated oven for 15 to 18 minutes or until golden brown.

variations

APPLE CINNAMON MUFFINS: Add 1 tsp (5 mL) cinnamon, 2 tbsp (25 mL) butter and 1 1/2 cups (375 mL) finely chopped apples.

BACON MUFFINS: Fry 5 strips side bacon until crisp; crumble. Set aside to cool. Substitute bacon and drippings for the melted butter.

BLUEBERRY MUFFINS: Substitute brown sugar for granulated sugar. Dredge 1 1/2 cups (375 mL) frozen blueberries in 2 tbsp (25 mL) of flour taken from Basic recipe. (This prevents blueberries from sinking). Fold berries into batter.

CHEESE MUFFINS: Add 1 cup (250 mL) grated sharp cheese to dry ingredients.

CORNMEAL MUFFINS: Use 3/4 cup (175 mL) cornmeal and 1 1/4 cups (300 mL) all-purpose flour instead of 2 cups (500 mL) all-purpose flour. Add 1 tbsp (15 mL) more granulated sugar (or omit sugar completely.) Use 1 egg instead of 2 eggs.

DOUBLE TOP MUFFINS: Place 1 cooked, dried apricot half in bottom of each greased muffin cup; fill two-thirds full with batter. Top with 1/2 cup (125 mL) firmly packed brown sugar, 1/2 cup (125 mL) softened butter or margarine, 1/3 cup (75 mL) all-purpose flour and 1 tsp (5 mL) cinnamon.

DRIED FRUIT AND NUT MUFFINS: Add 1/2 cup (125 mL) dried fruit (raisins, figs, chopped pitted dates) and/or nuts.

OATMEAL MUFFINS: Substitute 1 cup (250 mL) quick-cooking oats (uncooked) for 1 cup (250 mL) flour. Add 1/4 cup (50 mL) more flour.

ORANGE MUFFINS: Add 1 tbsp (15 mL) grated orange zest to dry ingredients. Substitute orange juice for milk.

PUMPKIN MUFFINS: Add 1 tsp (5 mL) cinnamon and 1/2 tsp (2 mL) nutmeg to dry ingredients. Add 2/3 cup (150 mL) canned pumpkin with the milk.

RICE MUFFINS: Use 1 cup (250 mL) flour and 1 cup (250 mL) cold boiled rice. Use 1 egg instead of 2 eggs and 2/3 cup (150 mL) milk instead of 1 cup (250 mL). Add rice last, mixing in lightly. Bake for about 30 minutes.

QUICK TEA CAKE MUFFINS: Increase sugar to 1/2 cup (125 mL) and eggs to 3 eggs. Reduce milk to 3/4 cup (175 mL). Bake at 425° F (220° C) for about 15 minutes.

rich biscuit-style muffins

Preheat oven to 400° F (200° C)
Muffin tin, greased

2 cups	all-purpose flour	500 mL
2 1/2 tsp	baking powder	12 mL
2 tbsp	granulated sugar	25 mL
1/2 tsp	salt	2 mL
1/2 cup	shortening	125 mL
1	egg, well beaten	1
3/4 cup	milk	175 mL

1. In a bowl sift together flour, baking powder, sugar and salt. Using a pastry blender, cut in shortening.

2. In another bowl combine egg and milk. Add to dry ingredients; stir until moistened. Spoon better into prepared muffin tin. Bake in preheated oven for 25 minutes.

variations

CRANBERRY-CUBE MUFFINS: Fill muffin tins one-third full. Cut 1 cup (250 mL) canned jellied cranberry sauce into 1/2-inch (1 cm) cubes. Sprinkle over batter. Spoon in remaining batter.

CHEESE-CARAWAY MUFFINS: Add 1 cup (250 mL) shredded sharp processed cheese and 1 tsp (5 mL) caraway seed to flour mixture.

BACON MUFFINS: Add 1/2 cup (125 mL) crumbled crisp bacon to dry ingredients.

RAISIN, NUT OR DATE MUFFINS: Add 1/2 to 3/4 cup (125 mL to 175 mL) raisins, chopped nuts or coarsely cut dates.

apple crunch muffins

Preheat oven to 375° F (190° C)
Muffin tin, greased

1 1/2 cups	all-purpose flour	375 mL
1/3 cup	granulated sugar	75 mL
2 tsp	baking powder	10 mL
1/2 tsp	salt	2 mL
1/2 cup	dry non-fat milk	125 mL
1 tsp	cinnamon	5 mL
1/4 cup	softened shortening	50 mL
1	egg	1
1/2 cup	water	125 mL
1 cup	finely chopped peeled apples	250 mL

TOPPING

| 1/3 cup | firmly packed brown sugar | 75 mL |
| 1/3 cup | finely chopped nuts | 75 mL |

1. In a bowl combine flour, sugar, baking powder, salt, milk and 1/2 tsp (2 mL) cinnamon; mix well. Add shortening, egg, water and apples. Mix quickly, just until blended. Spoon batter into prepared muffin tin, filling two-thirds full.

2. In a bowl combine remaining cinnamon, brown sugar and nuts; sprinkle over muffins. Bake in preheated oven for 20 to 25 minutes.

esther's special banana muffins

1 cup	granulated sugar	250 mL
2	eggs	2
1/2 cup	softened margarine	125 mL
2 cups	all-purpose flour	500 mL
2 tsp	baking soda	10 mL
3 or 4	medium bananas, mashed	3 or 4

Preheat oven to 425° F (220° C)
Large muffin tin, paper-lined

1. In a bowl cream together sugar and eggs until well mixed. Add margarine; blend well. Add flour and baking soda; mix until a loose dough forms.

2. Add bananas; stir just until moist. Spoon batter into prepared muffin tin, filling to top.

3. Bake in preheated oven for 15 to 20 minutes or until golden brown. After 15 minutes, turn pans around, back to front, for last 5 minutes of baking.

muffin stuff
I always mix batter in stainless steel bowls.
Ripe bananas are best to use.
If you plan to double the recipe, use only 1 1/2 cups (375 mL) sugar.

banana muffins plus

1 cup	granulated sugar	250 mL
1/2 cup	butter or shortening	125 mL
1	egg	1
3	mashed bananas	3
1/2 tsp	salt	2 mL
2 tbsp	orange juice or milk	25 mL
1 1/2 tsp	baking powder	7 mL
1/2 tsp	baking soda	2 mL
2 cups	all-purpose flour	500 mL
1/2 cup	chocolate chips (optional)	125 mL

Preheat oven to 350° F (180° C)
Muffin tin, greased or paper-lined

1. In a bowl cream together sugar, butter and egg; mix well. Add bananas, salt, orange juice, baking powder, baking soda, flour and chocolate chips; stir well.

2. Spoon batter into prepared muffin tin, filling to top. Bake in preheated oven for 20 to 30 minutes.

banana bran muffins

1/2 cup	granulated sugar	125 mL
1 cup	brown sugar	250 mL
1 cup	vegetable oil	250 mL
3	eggs	3
1 tsp	vanilla	5 mL
1 1/2 cups	mashed banana	375 mL
3 cups	natural bran	750 mL
1 1/2 cups	buttermilk	375 mL
3 cups	all-purpose flour	750 mL
3 tsp	baking powder	15 mL
3 tsp	baking soda	15 mL
1 tsp	salt	5 mL
1 cup	raisins	250 mL

Preheat oven to 375° F (190° C)
Muffin tin, greased or paper-lined

1. In a bowl combine granulated sugar, brown sugar and oil. Beat in eggs, one at a time. Add vanilla and banana; mix well. Add bran and buttermilk.

2. In another bowl combine flour, baking powder, baking soda and salt. Add to banana mixture; stir until ingredients are just mixed. Do not overmix. Fold in raisins.

3. Spoon batter into prepared muffin tin, filling to top. Bake in preheated oven for 15 to 20 minutes.

muffin stuff

This recipe makes about 30 to 36 muffins. If that's too many, feel free to halve the recipe. Or simply freeze the muffins and use as needed.

banana date-nut muffins

1	pkg. (7 oz [210 g]) bran muffin mix with dates *or* corn muffin mix	1
1 cup	mashed ripe bananas	250 mL
2	eggs	2
1/3 cup	chopped walnuts or pecans	75 mL

Preheat oven to 400° F (200° C)
Muffin tin, greased or paper-lined

1. In a bowl combine muffin mix, bananas, eggs and walnuts; mix just until blended.

2. Spoon batter into prepared muffin tin, filling to top. Bake in preheated oven for 15 to 20 minutes or until done.

variation

Use plain bran mix instead of bran muffin mix and add 1/2 cup (125 mL) chopped dates.

honey bran muffins

1 1/4 cups	all-purpose flour	300 mL
3/4 tsp	baking soda	4 mL
1/2 tsp	baking powder	2 mL
1/2 tsp	salt	2 mL
1 1/2 cups	bran flakes cereal	375 mL
1 1/4 cups	buttermilk	300 mL
1/4 cup	oil	50 mL
1/4 cup	honey	50 mL
1	egg	1
1/2 cup	dark raisins	125 mL

Preheat oven to 400° F (200° C)
12-cup muffin tin

1. In a bowl combine flour, baking soda, baking powder, salt and Bran flakes.

2. In another bowl combine buttermilk, oil, honey and egg; whisk well. Pour into flour mixture; stir just until moist and blended.

3. Fold in raisins. Spoon batter into muffin tin, filling three-quarters full. Bake in preheated oven for 15 to 20 minutes.

nutritious raisin bran muffins

1 cup	all-bran or natural bran cereal	250 mL
1 cup	milk	250 mL
1	egg	1
3 tbsp	butter or margarine or shortening, melted	45 mL
1 tsp	vanilla	5 mL
1 cup	raisins	250 mL
1 cup	all-purpose flour	250 mL
3 tsp	baking powder	15 mL
1/2 cup	brown sugar	125 mL
1 tsp	cinnamon	5 mL
1/2 tsp	salt	2 mL

Preheat oven to 400° F (200° C)
12-cup muffin tin, greased

1. In a bowl combine bran and milk. Add egg, butter and vanilla; mix well. Stir in raisins.

2. In another bowl sift together flour and baking powder. Add brown sugar, cinnamon and salt; mix well. Make a well in the center; add bran mixture. Stir just until blended.

3. Spoon batter into prepared muffin tin. Bake in preheated oven for 15 to 20 minutes.

esther's favorite blueberry muffins

Preheat oven to 400° F (200° C)
12-cup muffin tin, greased or paper-lined

1/4 cup	softened butter or margarine	50 mL
3/4 cup	granulated sugar	175 mL
1	egg, beaten	1
1 1/2 cups	pastry flour	375 mL
1/2 tsp	salt	2 mL
2 tsp	baking powder	10 mL
1/2 cup	milk	125 mL
1 cup	fresh or frozen blueberries	250 mL

1. In a bowl cream together butter and sugar. Add egg; mix well.

2. In another bowl sift together flour, salt and baking powder. Add to creamed mixture alternately with milk; stir just until moistened. Fold in blueberries.

3. Spoon batter into prepared muffin tin, filling to top. Bake in preheated oven for 15 to 20 minutes or until browned.

old-fashioned blueberry muffins

Preheat oven to 400° F (200° C)
12-cup muffin tin, greased or paper-lined

2	eggs	2
1 1/4 cups	milk	300 mL
1/2 cup	melted butter or margarine	125 mL
1 tsp	grated lemon zest	5 mL
1 1/2 cups	all-purpose flour	375 mL
1 cup	whole wheat flour	250 mL
1/2 cup	granulated sugar	125 mL
1 tbsp	baking powder	15 mL
1/2 tsp	salt	2 mL
1 1/2 cups	fresh or frozen blueberries	375 mL

1. In a bowl combine eggs, milk, butter and lemon zest; whisk well.

2. In another bowl combine all-purpose flour, whole wheat flour, sugar, baking powder and salt; mix well. Make a well in the center. Pour in egg mixture; stir just until ingredients are moistened.

3. Spoon batter into prepared muffin tin, dividing evenly. Bake in preheated oven for 15 to 20 minutes.

blueberry-orange muffins

Preheat oven to 350° F (180° C)
12-cup muffin tin, greased

1 3/4 cups	all-purpose flour	425 mL
1/2 cup	granulated sugar	125 mL
1 tsp	grated orange zest	5 mL
1 tbsp	baking powder	15 mL
1 cup	fresh or frozen blueberries	250 mL
1 cup	milk	250 mL
1/2 cup	melted butter	125 mL
1	egg	1
1/2 tsp	salt	2 mL
TOPPING		
2 tbsp	melted butter	25 mL
1/4 cup	orange juice	50 mL
1/4 cup	granulated sugar	50 mL

1. In a bowl sift together flour, sugar, orange zest and baking powder. Add blueberries; toss to combine well.

2. In another bowl whisk together milk, butter, egg and salt. Add to flour mixture; stir quickly just until all ingredients are moistened. Spoon batter into prepared muffin tin, dividing evenly. Bake in preheated oven for 15 to 18 minutes or until golden brown.

3. In a bowl combine butter and orange juice. Pour sugar into another bowl. When muffins are ready, remove from tins. Dip tops into butter mixture and then into sugar.

best-ever bran muffins

Preheat oven to 375° F (190° C)
18-cup muffin tin, greased

2 1/2 cups	all-purpose flour	625 mL
3/4 cup	brown sugar	175 mL
1 1/2 cups	natural bran	375 mL
1 1/2 tsp	cinnamon	7 mL
1 tsp	nutmeg	5 mL
2 tsp	baking soda	10 mL
1/2 tsp	salt	2 mL
2	eggs	2
3/4 cup	vegetable oil	175 mL
2 cups	buttermilk	500 mL
1/4 cup	molasses	50 mL
1 cup	raisins (dark or yellow)	250 mL

1. In a bowl combine flour, brown sugar, bran, cinnamon, nutmeg, baking soda and salt. Make a well in the center.

2. In another bowl whisk together eggs, oil, buttermilk and molasses. Pour into flour mixture; stir just until blended. Fold in raisins.

3. Spoon batter into prepared muffin tins, filling to top. Bake in preheated oven for 20 to 25 minutes.

CHOCOLATE CHIPIT SNACKIN' MUFFINS (PAGE 37) ➤

carrot pineapple streusel muffins

Preheat oven to 400° F (200° C)
12-cup muffin tin, greased or paper-lined

STREUSEL TOPPING

1/4 cup	lightly packed brown sugar	50 mL
1/4 cup	chopped walnuts	50 mL
1	pkg (15 oz [450 g]) carrot raisin loaf cake mix	1
1 cup	undrained crushed pineapple	250 mL
1	egg	1
3 tbsp	oil	45 mL

1. In a bowl combine sugar and walnuts; set aside.

2. In another bowl combine cake mix, pineapple, egg and oil; mix until smooth.

3. Spoon batter into prepared muffin tins, filling three-quarters full. Sprinkle with topping. Bake in preheated oven for 20 minutes.

muffin stuff
These are quick and easy to make – delicious!

creamy rice muffins

Preheat oven to 350° F (180° C)
Muffin tin, greased

2 cups	milk *or* water	500 mL
1 cup	rice (not instant) or 2 cups (500 mL) cooked rice	250 mL
4 tbsp	butter *or* margarine	60 mL
4 tbsp	granulated sugar	60 mL
2	eggs	2
1 cup	sour cream	250 mL
3/4 cup	all-purpose flour	175 mL
1 tsp	baking powder	5 mL
1/4 tsp	salt	1 mL

1. In a saucepan over medium-high heat, bring milk to a boil; add rice. Cook, covered, until thick and milk is absorbed. Set aside to cool.

2. In a bowl cream together butter, sugar, eggs and sour cream. Add flour, baking powder and salt; mix well. Add cooled rice; stir just until blended.

3. Spoon batter into prepared muffin tins, filling to top. Bake in preheated oven for about 45 minutes.

muffin stuff
Delicious served warm with sour cream and sliced strawberries.

◄ GOLDEN HONEY BRAN MUFFINS (PAGE 58)

carrot plus muffins

3 cups	all-purpose flour	750 mL
1 tsp	baking powder	5 mL
1/2 tsp	baking soda	2 mL
1/2 tsp	salt	2 mL
1/2 tsp	cloves	2 mL
1/2 tsp	nutmeg	2 mL
1 tbsp	chopped candied ginger	15 mL
1/2 cup	granulated sugar	125 mL
1/2 cup	brown sugar	125 mL
1/2 cup	vegetable oil	125 mL
2	eggs	2
1/2 cup	apricot juice *or* orange juice	125 mL
1	can (14 oz [425 g]) apricots, drained *or* 8 fresh ripe apricots, reserving some slices for topping	1
1 cup	grated carrots	250 mL
1 cup	grated rutabaga	250 mL
1/2 cup	chopped pecans	125 mL
TOPPING (optional)		
1	pkg (8 oz [250 g]) soft cream cheese	1
1/4 cup	apricot juice *or* orange juice	50 mL
1/2 cup	icing sugar	125 mL

Preheat oven to 400° F (200° C)
Muffin tin, greased

1. In a bowl combine 2 3/4 cups (675 mL) flour, baking powder, baking soda, salt, cloves and nutmeg.

2. In another bowl combine ginger and remaining flour; mix well. Add to clove mixture.

3. In another bowl combine granulated sugar, brown sugar and oil. Add eggs one at a time; whisk in juice. Pour into flour mixture, stirring just until moistened. Add apricots, carrots, rutabaga and pecans.

4. Spoon batter into prepared muffin tin, filling three-quarters full. Bake in preheated oven for 20 to 25 minutes or until toothpick inserted in center comes out clean.

5. In a bowl combine cream cheese, juice and icing sugar; mix well. Spread onto cooled muffins. Top with a slice of apricot.

muffin stuff

Rutabaga and carrots make a great combination. The end result is a dense, moist muffin.

special carrot puddings

3/4 cup	shortening	175 mL
1/2 cup	brown sugar	125 mL
1	egg	1
1 1/4 cups	all-purpose flour	300 mL
1/2 tsp	baking soda	2 mL
1 tsp	baking powder	5 mL
1 tsp	salt	5 mL
1 tbsp	water	15 mL
1 tbsp	lemon juice	15 mL
1 tsp	vanilla	5 mL
2 cups	grated carrots	500 mL

Preheat oven to 400° F (200° C)
Muffin tin, greased

1. In a bowl combine shortening and brown sugar; mix well. Add egg, flour, baking soda, baking powder, salt, water, lemon juice, vanilla and carrots. Do not overmix.

2. Heat prepared muffin tin in oven for a few minutes. Spoon in batter, filling cups to top. Bake in preheated oven for 20 minutes.

muffin stuff

I serve these with meat dinners or with a green salad.

esther's savory cheese muffins

2 cups	all-purpose flour	500 mL
3 tbsp	granulated sugar	45 mL
1 tbsp	baking powder	15 mL
1/2 tsp	grated lemon zest (optional)	2 mL
1	egg, slightly beaten	1
1 cup	milk	250 mL
1/4 cup	melted butter or margarine	50 mL
1 cup	shredded Cheddar cheese	250 mL

Preheat oven to 425° F (220° C)
Muffin tin, greased or paper-lined

1. In a bowl combine flour, sugar, baking powder and lemon zest. Make a well in center of mixture.

2. In another bowl combine egg, milk and butter; whisk well. Stir into flour mixture. Reserve 2 tbsp (25 mL) cheese for topping; add remaining cheese to flour mixture. Mix until moist and blended.

3. Spoon batter into prepared muffin tin, filling three-quarters full. Sprinkle tops with reserved cheese.

4. Bake in preheated oven for 20 minutes or until golden brown.

variations

The recipe did call for 3/4 tsp (4 mL) garlic salt. I don't use it, but you might want to give it a try.
You can replace the 1 cup (250 mL) milk with 1/2 cup (125 mL) milk and 1/2 cup (125 mL) plain yogurt.

cottage cheese muffins

1	pkg (12 oz [375 g]) dry cottage cheese	1
3 tbsp	granulated sugar	45 mL
2	eggs, slightly beaten	2
1/2 cup	melted butter or margarine	125 mL
Pinch	salt	Pinch
2 tsp	baking powder	10 mL
1 cup	all-purpose flour	250 mL

Preheat oven to 400° F (200° C)
Muffin tin, greased

1. In a bowl combine cottage cheese, sugar, eggs and butter; mix well. Add salt, baking powder and flour; stir just until blended.

2. Spoon batter into prepared muffin tin, filling three-quarters full. Bake in preheated oven for 20 to 25 minutes or until lightly browned.

muffin stuff

Delicious served warm with sour cream and thawed frozen strawberries.

variations

Use 2 cups (500 mL) dry cottage cheese and 1/2 cup (125 mL) creamed cottage cheese.

parmesan muffins

1	egg	1
1/2 cup	plain yogurt *or* sour cream	125 mL
1 cup	milk	250 mL
1/2 cup	melted butter or margarine	125 mL
2 1/2 cups	all-purpose flour	625 mL
1/2 cup	grated Parmesan cheese	125 mL
1/4 cup	granulated sugar	50 mL
1 tbsp	baking powder	15 mL
1 tsp	salt	5 mL
1/2 tsp	dried basil	2 mL

Preheat oven to 400° F (200° C)
12-cup muffin tin, greased or paper-lined

1. In a bowl combine egg, yogurt, milk and butter; whisk well.

2. In another bowl combine flour, cheese, sugar, baking powder, salt and basil. Make a well in center of mixture; pour in egg mixture. Stir just until blended.

3. Spoon batter into prepared muffin tin, dividing equally. Bake in preheated oven for about 20 minutes.

variations

Replace basil with 1/4 tsp (1 mL) rosemary. Add 4 tbsp (50 mL) yellow cornmeal to the dry ingredients.

Replace basil with package of fine herbs from a store-bought pizza mix.

chocolate cheesecake muffins

Preheat oven to 375° F (190° C)
Muffin tin, greased or paper-lined

FILLING

1	pkg (3 oz [75 g]) softened cream cheese	1
2 tbsp	granulated sugar	25 mL
1 cup	all-purpose flour	250 mL
1/2 cup	granulated sugar	125 mL
3 tbsp	unsweetened cocoa	45 mL
2 tsp	baking powder	10 mL
1/2 tsp	salt	2 mL
1	egg, beaten	1
3/4 cup	milk	175 mL
1/3 cup	oil	75 mL
	Icing sugar (optional)	

1. In a bowl combine cream cheese and sugar; beat until light and fluffy. Set aside.

2. In another bowl combine flour, sugar, cocoa, baking powder and salt. Make a well in center of mixture.

3. In another bowl combine egg, milk and oil. Pour into flour mixture; stir just until lumpy and moist.

4. Spoon batter into prepared muffin tin, filling cups half full. Add 1 tsp (5 mL) cheese filling; top with remaining batter.

5. Bake in preheated oven for 20 minutes. Dust with icing sugar, if desired.

chocolate chipit snackin' muffins

Preheat oven to 400° F (200° C)
Muffin tin, paper-lined

1 1/2 cups	all-purpose flour	375 mL
1 cup	granulated sugar	250 mL
2 tbsp	cocoa	25 mL
1 tsp	baking powder	5 mL
1 tsp	baking soda	5 mL
1/2 tsp	salt	2 mL
1/4 cup	oil	50 mL
1 tsp	vanilla	5 mL
1 tbsp	vinegar	15 mL
1 cup	warm water	250 mL
1/2 cup	chocolate chips	125 mL

1. In a bowl combine flour, sugar, cocoa, baking powder, baking soda and salt. Make a well in the center. Add oil, vanilla, vinegar and warm water. Stir just until moist. Add chocolate chips.

2. Spoon batter into prepared muffin tin, filling to top. Bake in preheated oven for 15 to 20 minutes.

variation
Before putting in oven, sprinkle chocolate chips over top.

chocolate date muffins

2 cups	all-purpose flour	500 mL
4 tsp	baking powder	20 mL
1/2 tsp	salt	2 mL
1/2 cup	granulated sugar	125 mL
1/2 cup	cocoa	125 mL
1/2 cup	sliced dates	125 mL
1 cup	milk	250 mL
1	egg, beaten	1
2 tbsp	shortening, melted	25 mL

Preheat oven to 350° F (180° C)
12-cup muffin tin, greased

1. In a bowl sift together flour, baking powder, salt, sugar and cocoa. Add dates; mix with your fingers. Add milk, egg and shortening; stir just until blended.

2. Spoon batter into prepared muffin tin, filling two-thirds full. Bake in preheated oven for 20 minutes.

chunky chocolate orange muffins

1/2 cup	softened butter	125 mL
1 cup	granulated sugar	250 mL
2	eggs	2
1/2 cup	sour cream	125 mL
	Grated zest of 2 oranges	
1/2 cup	orange juice	125 mL
2 cups	all-purpose flour *or* 2 1/4 cups (550 mL) cake and pastry flour	500 mL
1 tsp	baking powder	5 mL
1/2 tsp	baking soda	2 mL
3	squares semi-sweet chocolate, chopped *or* 1/2 cup (125 mL) chocolate chips	3
1	square semi-sweet chocolate, melted	1

Preheat oven to 400° F (200° C)
Muffin tin, greased

1. In a bowl combine butter and sugar; cream until light and fluffy. Add eggs one at a time; beat well. Add sour cream, orange zest and orange juice; mix well.

2. In another bowl combine flour, baking powder, baking soda and chopped chocolate. Add to creamed mixture; stir gently just until blended.

3. Spoon batter into prepared muffin tin, filling three-quarters full. Bake in preheated oven for 18 to 22 minutes or until top springs back when lightly touched. Set aside to cool. Drizzle with melted chocolate.

coffee cake muffins

TOPPING

1/3 cup	granulated sugar	75 mL
1 1/2 tsp	cinnamon	7 mL
1 tbsp	margarine, melted	15 mL
3 tbsp	softened butter	45 mL
3/4 cup	granulated sugar	175 mL
1	egg	1
2 cups	flour	500 mL
3 tsp	baking powder	15 mL
Pinch	salt	Pinch
3/4 cup	milk	175 mL
1 cup	raisins	250 mL

Preheat oven to 375° F (190° C)
Muffin tin, greased or paper-lined

1. In a bowl combine sugar, cinnamon and margarine; mix well. Set aside.

2. In another bowl beat butter. Add sugar and egg; beat well.

3. In another bowl combine flour, baking powder and salt. Add to creamed mixture alternately with milk; blend well. Fold in raisins.

4. Spoon batter into prepared muffin tin, dividing evenly. Sprinkle with topping. Bake in preheated oven for 20 minutes.

coffee walnut muffins

1 tbsp	instant coffee	15 mL
1/2 cup	hot water	125 mL
1/2 cup	milk or cream	125 mL
1	egg, beaten	1
1/2 cup	melted shortening or oil	125 mL
1 1/2 cups	all-purpose flour	375 mL
3 tsp	baking powder	15 mL
1/3 cup	granulated sugar	75 mL
1 tsp	salt	5 mL
1/2 cup	chopped walnuts	125 mL

Preheat oven to 375° F (190° C)
Muffin tin, greased

1. In a bowl dissolve coffee in hot water. Add milk, egg and shortening; stir to combine well.

2. In another bowl combine flour, baking powder, sugar and salt. Add walnuts; stir well. Add coffee mixture; stir just until moist.

3. Spoon batter into prepared muffin tin, dividing evenly. Bake in preheated oven for 15 to 20 minutes.

coffee-raisin spice muffins

Preheat oven to 400° F (200° C)
Muffin tin, paper-lined

TOPPING

1 cup	icing sugar	250 mL
2 to 3 tsp	grated lemon zest	10 to 15 mL
4 to 5 tsp	lemon juice	20 to 25 mL

1 cup	coffee	250 mL
1 cup	granulated sugar *or* packed brown sugar	250 mL
1 1/2 cups	chopped raisins	375 mL
1/3 cup	butter *or* margarine *or* shortening	75 mL
1/2 tsp	ground cloves	2 mL
1 tsp	cinnamon	5 mL
1 tsp	nutmeg	5 mL
1/2 tsp	salt	2 mL
1/2 tsp	baking powder	2 mL
1 tsp	baking soda	5 mL
2 cups	all-purpose flour	500 mL

1. In a bowl combine icing sugar, lemon zest and lemon juice; mix well. Set aside.

2. In a saucepan over medium-high heat combine coffee, sugar, raisins, butter, cloves, cinnamon and nutmeg; bring to a boil. Cook for 3 minutes. Set aside to cool.

3. When cool add salt, baking powder, baking soda and flour; mix well.

4. Spoon batter into prepared muffin tin, filling two-thirds full. Bake in preheated oven for 15 to 20 minutes or until toothpick inserted in center comes out clean. Set aside to cool. Drizzle with topping.

date muffins

Preheat oven to 400° F (200° C)
Muffin tin, greased

1/3 cup	shortening	75 mL
1	egg, beaten	1
3/4 cup	milk	175 mL
2 cups	all-purpose flour	500 mL
3 tsp	baking powder	15 mL
1/2 tsp	salt	2 mL
1 cup	chopped pitted dates	250 mL

1. In a bowl cream shortening. Add egg and milk; beat well.

2. In another bowl sift together flour, baking powder and salt. Add to creamed mixture; blend well. Add dates.

3. Spoon batter into prepared muffin tin, dividing evenly. Bake in preheated oven for about 25 minutes.

variation

For sweet muffins add 1/4 cup (50 mL) sugar.

sweet raisin muffins

1 cup	raisins	250 mL
1 tbsp	grated orange zest	15 mL
1 cup	boiling water	250 mL
1/2 tsp	baking soda	2 mL
1/2 cup	granulated sugar	125 mL
2 tbsp	margarine	25 mL
1	egg	1
1 3/4 cups	all-purpose flour	425 mL
2 tsp	baking powder	10 mL
1/2 tsp	cinnamon	2 mL
1/4 tsp	nutmeg	1 mL

Preheat oven to 425° F (220° C)
12-cup muffin tin, greased

1. In a bowl combine raisins and orange zest. Add boiling water and baking soda. Set aside to cool.

2. In another bowl cream together sugar and margarine. Add egg; beat well. Add raisin mixture; beat well.

3. In another bowl combine flour, baking powder, cinnamon and nutmeg. Fold into creamed mixture; stir just until moist.

4. Spoon batter into prepared muffin tin, filling three-quarters full. Bake in preheated oven for 20 minutes or until toothpick inserted in center comes out clean.

quick bake muffins

1 cup	quick-rising flour	250 mL
3 tbsp	mayonnaise	45 mL
1/2 cup	milk	125 mL

Preheat oven to 400° F (200° C)
Muffin tin, greased or paper-lined

1. In a bowl combine flour and mayonnaise. Add milk, a little at a time, stirring just until moistened.

2. Form dough into balls; place into prepared muffin tin. Bake in preheated oven for about 20 minutes.

muffin stuff
If you don't have quick-rising flour, use 1 1/2 tsp (7 mL) baking powder to 1 cup (250 mL) all-purpose flour.

jam-filled muffins

1 1/2 cups	all-purpose flour	375 mL
1/4 cup	granulated sugar	50 mL
2 tsp	baking powder	10 mL
1/2 tsp	baking soda	2 mL
1/2 tsp	salt	2 mL
1	egg	1
1/2 tsp	vanilla	2 mL
1/4 cup	butter or margarine, melted	50 mL
1 cup	plain yogurt	250 mL
1/4 cup	milk	50 mL
	Jam *or* jelly	
1/4 cup	nuts (optional)	50 mL

Preheat oven to 425° F (220° C)
Muffin tin, greased

1. In a large bowl combine flour, sugar, baking powder, baking soda and salt.

2. In another bowl beat together egg and vanilla. Add butter, yogurt and milk; mix well. Add to flour mixture; stir just until blended.

3. Spoon batter into prepared muffin tin, filling half full. Add 1 tsp (5 mL) of your favorite jam or jelly to each; top with remaining batter. Add nuts, if desired. Bake in preheated oven for 15 to 20 minutes.

lemon tea muffins

1 cup	cake and pastry flour *or* all-purpose flour	250 mL
1/2 cup	granulated sugar	125 mL
1 1/2 tsp	baking powder	7 mL
1 tsp	salt	5 mL
2	eggs	2
1/2 cup	lemon juice	125 mL
1/4 cup	melted margarine	50 mL
2 tsp	grated lemon zest	10 mL
TOPPING		
1/4 cup	melted margarine	50 mL
1 tbsp	lemon juice	15 mL
	Granulated sugar	

Preheat oven to 375° F (190° C)
Muffin tin, greased or paper-lined

1. In a bowl combine flour, sugar, baking powder and salt.

2. In another bowl whisk together eggs, lemon juice, margarine and lemon zest. Add to flour mixture; stir just until moist and blended.

3. Spoon batter into prepared muffin tin, filling to top. Bake in preheated oven for 15 to 20 minutes. Remove muffins from pan while still warm.

4. In a bowl combine margarine and lemon juice. Dip muffin tops in juice mixture; dip in sugar.

the muffin lady's special mincemeat muffins

3/4 cup	oil	175 mL
1 cup	granulated sugar	250 mL
2	eggs, beaten	2
2 cups	all-purpose flour	500 mL
1 cup	milk	250 mL
1 cup	all-bran cereal *or* whole bran cereal	250 mL
2 tsp	baking powder	10 mL
1 tsp	salt	5 mL
1 tsp	baking soda	5 mL
1 cup	mincemeat	250 mL

Preheat oven to 350° F (180° C)
24-cup muffin tin, greased or paper-lined

1. In a bowl combine oil, sugar, eggs, flour, milk, cereal, baking powder, salt, baking soda and mincemeat; mix well.

2. Spoon batter into prepared muffin tin, filling to top. Bake in preheated oven for 20 to 25 minutes.

muffin stuff

If you don't want to use all of the batter, it can be stored in the refrigerator for about 2 weeks.

golden oatmeal muffins

1 cup	rolled oats *or* quick-cooking oatmeal	250 mL
1 cup	buttermilk *or* sour cream	250 mL
1/2 cup	vegetable oil *or* melted shortening	125 mL
1/2 cup	firmly packed brown sugar	125 mL
1	egg, beaten	1
1 cup	all-purpose flour	250 mL
1 tsp	baking powder	5 mL
1/2 tsp	baking soda	2 mL
1 tsp	salt	5 mL

Preheat oven to 400° F (200° C)
Muffin tin, greased

1. In a bowl combine oats and buttermilk; let stand for 5 minutes. Add oil, brown sugar and egg.

2. In another bowl combine flour, baking powder, baking soda and salt. Add to oat mixture, stirring just until moistened.

3. Spoon batter into prepared muffin tin, filling to top. Bake in preheated oven for 15 to 20 minutes or until golden brown.

peanut butter muffins

1/3 cup + 2 tsp	self-rising flour	75 mL + 10 mL
1 tbsp	superfine sugar	15 mL
1/4 cup	skim milk	50 mL
1	egg, lightly beaten	1
3 tbsp	chunky-style peanut butter, room temperature	45 mL
1 tsp	margarine, melted	5 mL

Preheat oven to 400° F (200° C)
Muffin tin, paper-lined

1. In a bowl sift together flour and sugar. Add milk, egg, peanut butter and margarine; stir just until blended (batter will be lumpy.)

2. Spoon batter into prepared muffin tin, filling three-quarters full. Bake in preheated oven for 20 minutes or until toothpick inserted in center comes out clean.

muffin stuff

These muffins are great served with any flavor jam.

peanut butter crunch muffins

Preheat oven to 400° F (200° C)
Muffin tin, greased

TOPPING

3 tbsp	peanut butter	45 mL
4 tbsp	granulated sugar	60 mL
2 tbsp	all-purpose flour	25 mL
1/8 tsp	salt	0.5 mL
2 cups	all-purpose flour	500 mL
1 tbsp	baking powder	15 mL
1/2 tsp	salt	2 mL
2 tbsp	granulated sugar	25 mL
1	egg, beaten	1
1 cup	milk	250 mL
1/3 cup	melted butter or margarine	75 mL

1. In a bowl combine peanut butter, sugar, flour and salt; mix with a fork. Set aside.

2. In another bowl combine flour, baking powder, salt and sugar. Make a well in the center.

3. In another bowl whisk together egg, milk and butter. Add to dry ingredients; stir quickly just until blended.

4. Spoon batter into prepared muffin tin, filling two-thirds full. Sprinkle with topping. Bake in preheated oven for 20 minutes.

peanut butter jelly muffins

1 1/2 cups	all-purpose flour	375 mL
1/2 cup	brown sugar	125 mL
1 tsp	baking powder	5 mL
1/2 tsp	baking soda	2 mL
1/2 tsp	salt	2 mL
1/2 cup	smooth peanut butter	125 mL
2	eggs, beaten	2
3/4 cup	milk	175 mL
1 tsp	vanilla	5 mL
4 tbsp	margarine, melted	60 mL
	Grape jelly	
	Apricot jam	

Preheat oven to 375° F (190° C)
Muffin tin, greased

1. In a bowl sift together flour, brown sugar, baking powder, baking soda and salt. Make a well in the center.

2. In another bowl combine peanut butter and eggs; beat well. Add milk, vanilla and margarine; mix thoroughly. Add to dry ingredients; mix until moist.

3. Spoon batter into prepared muffin tin, filling three-quarters full. Make an indentation in the center of each; spoon 1 tsp (5 mL) either grape jelly or apricot jam into each muffin. Bake in preheated oven for about 20 minutes.

muffin stuff

The contrasting colors of grape and apricot make a sweet, colorful arrangement.

pecan muffins

1 1/2 cups	all-purpose flour	375 mL
1/2 cup	granulated sugar	125 mL
1/2 cup	chopped pecans	125 mL
2 tsp	baking powder	10 mL
1/2 tsp	salt	2 mL
1	egg, slightly beaten	1
1/2 cup	milk	125 mL
1/4 cup	vegetable oil	50 mL

Preheat oven to 400° F (200° C)
Muffin tin, greased or paper-lined

1. In a bowl combine flour, sugar, pecans, baking powder and salt. Make a well in the center.

2. In another bowl combine egg, milk and oil. Add to dry ingredients; stir just until moist.

3. Spoon batter into prepared muffin tin, filling two-thirds full. Bake in preheated oven for 15 to 20 minutes.

mom's old-fashioned oatmeal muffins

1 1/2 cups	quick oatmeal	375 mL
1 cup	all-purpose flour	250 mL
1 tsp	baking powder	5 mL
1 tsp	baking soda	5 mL
1/2 tsp	salt	2 mL
1 tsp	cinnamon	5 mL
3/4 cup	brown sugar	175 mL
1	egg, lightly beaten	1
1/4 cup	oil	50 mL
1 cup	plain yogurt	250 mL
1/2 cup	raisins	125 mL

Preheat oven to 350° F (180° C)
Muffin tin, greased

1. In a bowl combine oatmeal, flour, baking powder, baking soda, salt, cinnamon and brown sugar. Make a well in the center.

2. In another bowl, whisk together egg, oil and yogurt. Add to dry ingredients; stir just until blended. Fold in raisins.

3. Spoon batter into prepared muffin tin. Bake in preheated oven for 20 to 25 minutes.

esther's famous poppyseed muffins

1/4 cup	vegetable oil	50 mL
3/4 cup	granulated sugar	175 mL
2	eggs	2
1/2 cup	poppy seeds	125 mL
1 cup	sour cream	250 mL
1/4 cup	milk	50 mL
2 cups	all-purpose flour	500 mL
1/2 tsp	baking soda	2 mL
2 tsp	baking powder	10 mL
1/2 tsp	salt	2 mL

Preheat oven to 425° F (220° C)
12-cup muffin tin, paper-lined

1. In a bowl cream together oil, sugar and eggs. Add poppy seeds, sour cream, milk, flour, baking soda, baking powder and salt. Stir just until moist and still lumpy. The mixture will be quite thick and heavy.

2. Spoon batter into prepared muffin tin, filling to top. Bake in preheated oven for 15 to 20 minutes or until toothpick inserted in center comes out clean.

poppyseed muffins

1 cup	milk	250 mL
1/2 cup	poppy seeds	125 mL
1/4 cup	butter *or* margarine	50 mL
3 tbsp	granulated sugar	45 mL
1	egg	1
1 tsp	vanilla	5 mL
2 cups	all-purpose flour	500 mL
3 tsp	baking powder	15 mL
3/4 tsp	salt	4 mL

Preheat oven to 400° F (200° C)
Muffin tin, greased

1. In a bowl combine milk and poppy seeds. Let stand for about 10 minutes.

2. In another bowl combine butter, sugar and egg; beat well. Add vanilla; blend thoroughly. Add poppy seed mixture.

3. In another bowl combine flour, baking powder and salt; mix thoroughly. Make a well in the center. Add liquid ingredients; stir just until moist.

4. Spoon batter into prepared muffin tin, filling three-quarters full. Bake in preheated oven for 20 to 25 minutes. Serve warm.

muffin stuff

Here is another version of poppy seed muffins that I know you'll enjoy.

pumpkin muffins

1	can (14 oz [398 mL]) pumpkin	1
4	eggs	4
1 1/2 cups	granulated sugar	375 mL
1 1/2 cups	oil	375 mL
3 cups	all-purpose flour	750 mL
3 tsp	cinnamon	15 mL
2 tsp	baking soda	10 mL
2 tsp	baking powder	10 mL
1 tsp	salt	5 mL
1 cup	raisins	250 mL

Preheat oven to 400° F (200° C)
Muffin tin, greased

1. In a bowl combine pumpkin and eggs. Add sugar and oil; mix well.

2. In another bowl combine flour, cinnamon, baking soda, baking powder, salt and raisins. Add to pumpkin mixture, stirring just until blended.

3. Spoon batter into prepared muffin tin, filling to top. Bake in preheated oven for 20 to 25 minutes.

muffin stuff

Most of the time I try to reduce the amount of sugar and oil used to 1 cup (250 mL) or less.

the muffin lady's famous rhubarb muffins

1 1/2 cups	brown sugar	375 mL
1/4 cup	oil	50 mL
2	eggs	2
2 tsp	vanilla	10 mL
1 cup	buttermilk	250 mL
1 1/2 cups	finely diced rhubarb	375 mL
1/2 cup	chopped walnuts or pecans	125 mL
2 1/2 cups	all-purpose flour	625 mL
1 tsp	baking powder	5 mL
1 tsp	baking soda	5 mL
1/2 tsp	salt	2 mL
TOPPING		
1/3 cup	granulated sugar	75 mL
1 1/2 tsp	cinnamon	7 mL
1 tbsp	margarine, melted	15 mL

Preheat oven to 425° F (220° C)
Muffin tin, greased or paper-lined

1. In a bowl whisk together brown sugar, oil, eggs and vanilla; mix well. Add buttermilk, rhubarb and walnuts.

2. In another bowl combine flour, baking powder, baking soda and salt. Add to rhubarb mixture; stir just until moist.

3. In another bowl combine sugar, cinnamon and margarine.

4. Spoon batter into prepared muffin tin, filling three-quarters full. Sprinkle with topping. Bake in preheated oven for about 20 minutes.

raisin muffins

1 cup	raisins	250 mL
1 1/2 cups	water	375 mL
2/3 cup	brown sugar	160 mL
1/2 cup	shortening	125 mL
1	egg, beaten	1
1 tsp	vanilla	5 mL
1 1/2 cups	all-purpose flour	375 mL
1 tsp	salt	5 mL
1 tsp	baking soda	5 mL
1 tsp	baking powder	5 mL

Preheat oven to 350° F (180° C)
Muffin tin, greased or paper-lined

1. In a saucepan over medium-high heat, combine raisins and water; bring to a boil. Cook for 20 minutes. Set aside to cool (keep in water).

2. In a bowl cream together brown sugar, shortening and egg. Add cooled raisins with water and vanilla.

3. In another bowl sift together flour, salt, baking soda and baking powder. Add to creamed mixture; stir just until blended.

4. Spoon batter into prepared muffin tin. Bake in preheated oven for about 20 minutes.

spicy raisin muffins

1 1/2 cups	raisins	375 mL
1 cup	water	250 mL
1/2 cup	brown sugar	125 mL
1/2 cup	butter or margarine	125 mL
1	egg, beaten	1
1 1/2 cups	all-purpose flour	375 mL
1 tsp	baking soda	5 mL
1/4 tsp	mace	1 mL
1 tsp	cinnamon	5 mL
1/4 tsp	cloves	1 mL

Preheat oven to 350° F (180° C)
16-cup muffin tin, greased or paper-lined

1. In a saucepan over medium-high heat, bring raisins and water to a boil. Simmer for 20 minutes. Set aside to cool. Retain 3/4 cup (175 mL) water; discard rest.

2. In a bowl cream together brown sugar and butter. Add egg and raisin water; beat well. Add raisins, flour, baking soda, mace, cinnamon and cloves; stir just until blended.

3. Spoon batter into prepared muffin tin, filling to top. Bake in preheated oven for about 15 minutes.

raisin nut muffins

1/2 cup	softened butter	125 mL
1 cup	granulated sugar	250 mL
3	eggs	3
2 cups	all-purpose flour	500 mL
2 tsp	baking powder	10 mL
1/4 tsp	nutmeg	1 mL
2/3 cup	milk	150 mL
1 cup	chopped walnuts	250 mL
1 cup	raisins, dredged in flour	250 mL

Preheat oven to 400° F (200° C)
Muffin tin, greased or paper-lined

1. In a bowl cream butter. Add sugar; beat slowly until well blended.

2. In another bowl beat eggs until light. Add to creamed mixture.

3. In another bowl sift together flour, baking powder and nutmeg. Add to batter alternately with milk; mix well. Fold in walnuts and raisins.

4. Spoon batter into prepared muffin tin, filling two-thirds full. Bake in preheated oven for 15 to 20 minutes.

rice pudding muffins

1 1/2 cups	all-purpose flour	375 mL
1/4 cup	granulated sugar	50 mL
1 1/2 tsp	baking powder	7 mL
1/2 tsp	baking soda	2 mL
1/4 tsp	salt	1 mL
1 tsp	cinnamon	5 mL
1 tsp	nutmeg	5 mL
1 cup	cooked white rice, cooled	250 mL
1	egg	1
2 tbsp	butter, melted	25 mL
1 1/4 cups	buttermilk	300 mL
	Confectioner's sugar	

Preheat oven to 400° F (200° C)
Muffin tin, greased

1. In a bowl combine flour, sugar, baking powder, baking soda, salt, cinnamon and nutmeg. Add rice.

2. In another bowl whisk together egg, butter and buttermilk. Add to flour mixture; stir just until moist.

3. Spoon batter into prepared muffin tin, dividing evenly. Bake in preheated oven for 15 to 20 minutes. Remove from tins; sprinkle with confectioner's sugar.

self-iced muffins

1 cup	brown sugar	250 mL
1 cup	margarine	250 mL
2 cups	all-purpose flour	500 mL
1	egg, beaten	1
1 cup	milk	250 mL
1 tsp	vinegar	5 mL
1 tsp	baking soda	5 mL
1 cup	dates, dredged in flour	250 mL
1 cup	raisins, dredged in flour	250 mL
1 tsp	cinnamon	5 mL
1 tsp	vanilla	5 mL

Preheat oven to 375° F (190° C)
Muffin tin, paper-lined

1. In a bowl combine sugar and margarine; beat well. Add flour. Set aside 3/4 cup (175 mL) of this mixture for topping.

2. To remaining mixture add egg, milk, vinegar and baking soda; combine well. Add dates, raisins, cinnamon and vanilla.

3. Spoon batter into prepared muffin tin, filling two-thirds full. Sprinkle with reserved mixture. Bake in preheated oven for 20 to 30 minutes.

southern biscuit muffins

2 1/2 cups	all-purpose flour	625 mL
1/4 cup	granulated sugar	50 mL
1 1/2 tbsp	baking powder	20 mL
3/4 cup	chilled butter or margarine	175 mL
1 cup	cold milk	250 mL

Preheat oven to 400° F (200° C)
12-cup muffin tin, greased

1. In a bowl combine flour, sugar and baking powder. Add butter; mix until crumbly. Add milk; stir just until moist.

2. Spoon batter into prepared muffin tin, dividing evenly. Bake in preheated oven for 20 minutes or until golden brown.

muffin stuff
Delicious with jam, jelly or honey, these muffins are just like baking powder biscuits.

sour cream raisin bran muffins

4 oz	butter *or* margarine	125 g
3/4 cup	brown sugar	175 mL
1	egg, slightly beaten	1
1 cup	all-purpose flour	250 mL
1/2 tsp	baking soda	2 mL
1/2 cup	bran flour *or* natural bran	125 mL
1 cup	sour cream	250 mL
1 tsp	vanilla	5 mL
3/4 cup	raisins	175 mL

Preheat oven to 375° F (190° C)
Muffin tin, greased or paper-lined

1. In a bowl cream together butter, brown sugar and egg. Add all-purpose flour, baking soda, bran flour, sour cream, vanilla and raisins; stir just until moist and blended.

2. Spoon batter into prepared muffin tin, filling to top. Bake in preheated oven for 20 to 25 minutes.

wheat germ muffins

2 cups	all-purpose flour	500 mL
2 tbsp	baking powder	25 mL
1 tsp	baking soda	5 mL
1 1/2 cups	wheat germ	375 mL
1 cup	firmly packed brown sugar	250 mL
2	eggs	2
1 1/2 cups	milk	375 mL
1/2 cup	vegetable oil	125 mL

Preheat oven to 400° F (200° C)
Muffin tin, greased or paper-lined

1. In a bowl combine flour, baking powder, baking soda, wheat germ and brown sugar; mix until well blended.

2. In another bowl whisk together eggs, milk and oil. Pour into dry ingredients; stir just until blended.

3. Spoon batter into prepared muffin tin, dividing evenly. Bake in preheated oven for 15 to 20 minutes.

wholesome wheat germ muffins

1 1/2 cups	all-purpose flour	375 mL
1/4 cup	brown sugar	50 mL
3 tsp	baking powder	15 mL
1/2 tsp	salt	2 mL
2/3 cup	wheat germ	160 mL
1/2 cup	raisins	125 mL
1 cup	milk	250 mL
1	egg	1
2 tbsp	melted margarine, cooled	25 mL

Preheat oven to 400° F (200° C)
12-cup muffin tin, greased

1. In a bowl combine flour, brown sugar, baking powder and salt; mix well. Add wheat germ and raisins.

2. In another bowl whisk together milk, egg and margarine. Add to dry ingredients; stir just until moistened. Do not overmix.

3. Spoon batter into prepared muffin tin, filling three-quarters full. Bake in preheated oven for about 20 minutes.

muffin stuff

Here's another wheat germ recipe. The raisins add a nice sweetness.

refrigerator muffins

all-bran breakfast muffins

1 cup	branflakes cereal	250 mL
1 cup	boiling water	250 mL
2 1/2 cups	all-purpose flour	625 mL
2 1/2 tsp	baking soda	12 mL
1 tsp	salt	5 mL
1/2 cup	shortening	125 mL
1 cup	granulated sugar	250 mL
2	eggs	2
2 1/2 cups	buttermilk	625 mL
2 cups	all-bran cereal	500 mL
1 cup	raisins	250 mL

Muffin tin, greased or paper-lined

1. In a bowl combine cereal and boiling water. Set aside to cool.

2. In another bowl combine flour, baking soda and salt. Set aside.

3. In another bowl cream together shortening and sugar. Add eggs, one at a time, beating well each time. Add dry ingredients to this mixture alternatively with buttermilk; stir until blended.

4. Add cooled bran bud mixture, All-Bran cereal and raisins; cover bowl tightly. Let stand overnight in refrigerator; do not stir. Spoon batter into prepared muffin tin. Bake at 400° F (200° C) for 30 minutes.

muffin stuff

This batter will keep for 3 to 4 weeks in the refrigerator if covered tightly.

applesauce whole wheat muffins

3/4 cup	all-purpose flour	175 mL
1/2 cup	whole wheat flour	125 mL
1 cup	uncooked quick-cooking rolled oats	250 mL
1/2 cup	packed brown sugar	125 mL
1 tsp	baking powder	5 mL
1/2 tsp	baking soda	2 mL
1/2 tsp	cinnamon	2 mL
1/4 tsp	salt	1 mL
3/4 cup	buttermilk	175 mL
1/4 cup	applesauce	50 mL
1/4 cup	vegetable oil	50 mL
1	egg, beaten	1
1/4 cup	raisins	50 mL

Muffin tin, greased or paper-lined

1. In a bowl combine all-purpose flour, whole wheat flour, oats, brown sugar, baking powder, baking soda, cinnamon and salt.

2. In a bowl combine buttermilk, applesauce, oil and egg; mix well. Add to dry ingredients; stir just until moistened. Fold in raisins. Cover bowl tightly; refrigerate overnight.

3. Spoon batter into prepared muffin tin. Bake at 400° F (200° C) for 18 to 20 minutes.

muffin stuff

Batter will keep, refrigerated, for 2 to 3 weeks.

blueberry bran muffins

Muffin tin, paper-lined

6	eggs	6
1 1/2 cups	firmly packed dark brown sugar	375 mL
1/4 cup	light molasses	50 mL
1/4 cup	honey	50 mL
4 cups	buttermilk	1 L
1 1/2 cups	vegetable oil	375 mL
1 tsp	vanilla	5 mL
2 1/2 cups	unprocessed bran flakes	625 mL
2 cups	wheat germ	500 mL
1 3/4 cups	finely chopped pecans or walnuts	425 mL
2 cups	fresh or frozen blue-berries, partially thawed	500 mL
4 1/2 cups	all-purpose flour	1.125 L
4 tsp	baking powder	20 mL
4 tsp	baking soda	20 mL
1 tsp	cinnamon	5 mL
1/4 tsp	salt	1 mL

1. In a bowl beat together eggs, brown sugar, molasses and honey until well blended. Add buttermilk, oil and vanilla; stir well. Add bran, wheat germ and 1 1/4 cups (300 mL) pecans. Let stand for 10 minutes; stir in berries.

2. In another bowl, combine flour, baking powder, baking soda, cinnamon and salt. Add to batter, mixing just until blended. Cover bowl tightly; refrigerate overnight.

3. Spoon batter into prepared muffin tin. Sprinkle tops evenly with remaining pecans. Bake at 400° F (200° C) for about 25 minutes.

muffin stuff
Batter can be stored in the refrigerator or frozen.

coffee n' bran muffins

Muffin tin, greased or paper-lined

1/2 cup	butter or margarine, soft or melted	125 mL
1 cup	granulated sugar	250 mL
2	eggs	2
1 cup	black coffee	250 mL
2 cups	buttermilk	500 mL
2 1/2 cups	all-purpose flour	625 mL
2 1/2 tsp	baking soda	12 mL
3 cups	wheat bran cereal	750 mL

1. In a bowl whisk together butter, sugar and eggs. Add coffee and buttermilk; whisk until mixture looks curdled. Add flour and baking soda; beat to blend well. Stir in bran. Cover bowl tightly; refrigerate.

2. When ready to bake, stir mixture well. Spoon batter into prepared muffin tin. Bake at 400° F (200° C) for 20 minutes.

golden honey bran muffins

Muffin tin, greased or paper-lined

6 cups	all-bran cereal	1.5 L
2 cups	boiling water	500 mL
1 cup	honey	250 mL
5 cups	all-purpose flour	1.25 L
2 tbsp	baking soda	25 mL
2 tsp	cinnamon	10 mL
1 tsp	salt	5 mL
1 cup	shortening	250 mL
1 cup	granulated sugar	250 mL
1 cup	lightly packed brown sugar	250 mL
4	eggs	4
4 cups	buttermilk	1 L
2 cups	raisins *or* chopped dates	500 mL

1. In a bowl cover bran cereal with boiling water. Add honey; stir well. Set aside.

2. In another bowl combine flour, baking soda, cinnamon and salt.

3. In another bowl cream together shortening, granulated sugar, brown sugar, eggs, buttermilk and soaked cereal. Add flour mixture; mix well. Stir in raisins. Pour batter into a container; cover tightly. Store in refrigerator for up to 2 months.

4. When ready to bake, spoon batter into prepared muffin tin, filling three-quarters full. Bake at 375° F (190° C) for 20 to 25 minutes.

convenient raisin bran muffins

Muffin tin, greased or paper-lined

1 cup	natural bran	250 mL
1 cup	boiling water	250 mL
1/2 cup	butter *or* margarine	125 mL
3/4 cup	brown sugar	175 mL
3	eggs	3
2 1/2 cups	all-purpose flour	625 mL
2 1/2 tsp	baking soda	12 mL
1/2 tsp	salt	2 mL
2 cups	risin bran cereal	500 mL
2 cups	buttermilk	500 mL
1 cup	raisins	250 mL
1 cup	coarsely chopped walnuts	250 mL

1. In a bowl cover bran with boiling water; set aside 20 minutes.

2. In a food processor combine butter, brown sugar, eggs and soaked bran; process until smooth.

3. In a bowl combine bran mixture, flour, baking soda, salt, cereal and buttermilk; beat well. Fold in raisins and walnuts.

4. Pour batter into a container; cover tightly. Store in the refrigerator for up to 6 weeks.

5. When ready to bake, spoon batter into prepared muffin tin, filling three-quarters full. Bake at 375° F (190° C) for 20 minutes.

oat bran refrigerator muffins

2/3 cup	wheat germ	150 mL
1 1/2 cups	natural bran	375 mL
1 1/2 cups	uncooked oat bran	375 mL
3 cups	all-bran cereal	750 mL
3 cups	boiling water	750 mL
1 cup	margarine	250 mL
1 cup	firmly packed brown sugar	250 mL
1/2 cup	granulated sugar	125 mL
1/2 cup	molasses	125 mL
4	eggs	4
4 cups	buttermilk	1 L
2 cups	raisins and/or dates	500 mL
3 cups	all-purpose flour	750 mL
2 cups	whole wheat flour	500 mL
3 tbsp	baking soda	45 mL
1 tsp	salt	5 mL

Muffin tin, greased or paper-lined

1. In a bowl combine wheat germ, natural bran, oat bran and bran cereal. Add boiling water; mix well. Set aside to cool.

2. In another bowl cream together margarine, brown sugar and granulated sugar; add molasses. Beat in eggs one at a time. Add buttermilk; mix well. Stir in raisins.

3. In another bowl combine all-purpose flour, whole wheat flour, baking soda and salt. Add to creamed mixture; mix well. Stir in bran mixture; blend well.

4. Pour batter into a container; cover tightly. Store in the refrigerator for at least 24 hours before baking.

5. When ready to bake, spoon batter into prepared muffin tin, filling three-quarters full. Bake at 375° F (190° C) for 25 to 30 minutes.

oldtime six week bran muffins

4 cups	bran	1 L
2 cups	bran flakes cereal	500 mL
2 cups	boiling water	500 mL
1 cup	butter	250 mL
1 cup	granulated sugar	250 mL
2 cups	brown sugar	500 mL
4	eggs	4
4 cups	buttermilk	1 L
1/2 cup	molasses	125 mL
5 cups	flour	1.25 L
2 tbsp	baking soda	25 mL
1 tbsp	baking powder	15 mL
1 tsp	salt	5 mL
2 cups	raisins	500 mL

Muffin tin, greased or paper-lined

1. In a bowl combine bran and bran flakes. Cover with boiling water; mix well. Set aside.

2. In another bowl cream together butter, granulated sugar and brown sugar. Beat in eggs one at a time. Add buttermilk and molasses; mix well.

3. In another bowl combine flour, baking soda, baking powder, salt and raisins. Add to buttermilk mixture; stir just until blended. Add bran mixture; mix well.

4. Pour batter into a container; cover tightly. Store in the refrigerator for up to 6 weeks.

5. When ready to bake, spoon batter into prepared muffin tin, filling three-quarters full. Bake at 400° F (200° C) for 20 to 25 minutes or until firm and springy to the touch.

pineapple bran muffins

2 cups	all-bran cereal	500 mL
2 cups	buttermilk	500 mL
2	eggs, slightly beaten	2
1	can 19 oz (540 mL) crushed pineapple, not drained	1
1/2 cup	melted butter or margarine	125 mL
2 1/2 cups	all-purpose flour	625 mL
3/4 cup	packed dark brown sugar	175 mL
2 tsp	salt	10 mL
2 tsp	baking soda	10 mL
1 cup	toasted chopped almonds	250 mL

Muffin tin, greased

1. In a bowl combine bran and buttermilk; let stand for 5 minutes. Add eggs, pineapple and butter; stir well.

2. In another bowl combine flour, brown sugar, salt, baking soda and almonds. Add to bran mixture; stir just until blended (batter will be lumpy.)

3. Pour batter into a container; cover tightly. Store in the refrigerator for up to 3 weeks.

4. When ready to bake, spoon batter into prepared muffin tin, filling three-quarters full. Bake at 375° F (190° C) for 25 minutes.

wholesome healthy

muffins

basic bran muffin

1 cup	all-purpose flour	250 mL
1/2 cup	packed brown sugar	125 mL
1/4 tsp	salt	1 mL
1 1/2 tsp	baking powder	7 mL
1/2 tsp	baking soda	2 mL
1 1/2 cups	natural bran	375 mL
1/2 cup	raisins	125 mL
1/2 cup	chopped nuts (optional)	125 mL
2	eggs, beaten	2
1 cup	milk	250 mL
1/4 cup	molasses	50 mL
1/2 cup	margarine, melted	125 mL

Preheat oven to 400° F (200° C)
12-cup muffin tin, greased or paper-lined

1. In a bowl combine flour, brown sugar, salt, baking powder, baking soda, bran, raisins and nuts. Make a well in the center.

2. In another bowl beat together eggs, milk, molasses and margarine. Add to flour mixture; stir just until moistened. Do not overmix (batter will be lumpy.)

3. Spoon batter into prepared muffin tins, dividing evenly. Bake in preheated oven for 18 to 20 minutes.

variations

BANANA BRAN: Replace molasses and raisins with 1 cup (250 mL) mashed bananas. Decrease milk to 1/2 cup (125 mL) and add 1 tsp (5 mL) cinnamon.

APPLESAUCE BRAN: Replace molasses with 3/4 cup (175 mL) applesauce. Decrease milk to 1/2 cup (125 mL) and add 1 tsp (5 mL) cinnamon or nutmeg.

CARROT BRAN: Add 1 cup (250 mL) grated carrots and 1 tsp (5 mL) cinnamon to dry ingredients.

all-bran cereal muffins

1 cup	all-bran cereal	250 mL
1 cup	milk	250 mL
1	egg	1
1/4 cup	melted shortening	50 mL
1/2 cup	raisins or chopped dates	125 mL
1 cup	all-purpose flour	250 mL
2 1/2 tsp	baking powder	12 mL
1/2 tsp	salt	2 mL
1/4 cup	granulated sugar	50 mL
1 tsp	cinnamon	5 m L
1/2 tsp	nutmeg	2 mL

Preheat oven to 400° F (200° C)
12-muffin tin, greased

1. In a bowl combine cereal and milk; mix well. Let stand until milk is absorbed. Add egg and shortening; beat well. Stir in raisins.

2. In another bowl sift together flour, baking powder, salt, sugar, cinnamon and nutmeg. Add to cereal mixture; blend well.

3. Spoon batter into prepared muffin tin, dividing evenly. Bake in preheated oven for 20 to 25 minutes.

SPICED CARROT BRAN MUFFINS (PAGE 67) ➤

apple bran muffins

1 cup	all-purpose flour	250 mL
1 tsp	baking soda	5 mL
1 tsp	baking powder	5 mL
1/2 tsp	salt	2 mL
3 tbsp	brown sugar	45 mL
1 cup	natural bran	250 mL
1	egg	1
1 cup	buttermilk *or* sour milk	250 mL
1/4 cup	vegetable oil	50 mL
2 tbsp	molasses	25 mL
1	small apple, peeled and finely chopped	1

Preheat oven to 400° F (200° C)
12-cup muffin tin, greased

1. In a bowl combine flour, baking soda, baking powder, salt and sugar; mix well. Add bran; stir well with a fork. Make a well in the center.

2. In another bowl beat together egg, buttermilk, oil and molasses; add apple. Pour into dry ingredients; stir just until blended.

3. Spoon batter into prepared muffin tin, dividing evenly. Bake in preheated oven for about 15 minutes.

applesauce bran muffins

3 cups	applesauce	750 mL
2 cups	buttermilk *or* sour milk	500 mL
1 cup	packed brown sugar	250 mL
3/4 cup	molasses	175 mL
3/4 cup	vegetable oil	175 mL
1 tbsp	vanilla	15 mL
3	eggs	3
3 cups	natural bran	750 mL
6 cups	all-purpose flour	1.5 L
1 tbsp	baking soda	15 mL
1 tbsp	cinnamon	15 mL
1 tbsp	salt	15 mL
3 cups	raisins *or* chopped dates	750 mL

Preheat oven to 375° F (190° C)
Muffin tin, greased

1. In a bowl whisk together applesauce, buttermilk, brown sugar, molasses, oil, vanilla and eggs. Stir in bran; let stand for 5 to 10 minutes.

2. In another bowl combine flour, baking soda, cinnamon and salt; mix well. Add applesauce mixture; stir just until blended. Fold in raisins.

3. Spoon batter into prepared muffin tin, filling to top (makes about 36 muffins; bake in batches.) Bake in preheated oven for about 25 minutes.

◄ BLUEBERRY MUFFINS (PAGE 103)

easy breakfast bran muffins

1 cup	natural bran	250 mL
1/2 cup	granulated sugar	125 mL
1 cup	all-purpose flour	250 mL
1 tsp	baking powder	5 mL
1 tsp	baking soda	5 mL
1/2 tsp	salt	2 mL
1	egg	1
6 tbsp	oil	90 mL
1 cup	boiling water	250 mL
1/3 cup	raisins *or* dates	75 mL

Preheat oven to 375° F (190° C)
Muffin tin, paper-lined

1. In a bowl combine bran, sugar, flour, baking powder, baking soda and salt. Make a well in the center.

2. In another bowl beat together egg and oil. Add raisins and boiling water; mix well. Pour into dry ingredients; stir just until blended.

3. Spoon batter into prepared muffin tin. Bake in preheated oven for about 20 to 25 minutes.

surprise brownie muffins

1 3/4 cups	all-purpose flour	425 mL
5 tsp	baking powder	25 mL
1 tsp	salt	5 mL
1 cup	granulated sugar (can be reduced to 1/2 cup [125 mL] or to taste)	250 mL
2/3 cup	cocoa or carob powder	150 mL
1 1/4 cups	natural bran	300 mL
2	eggs, beaten	2
1 cup	milk	250 mL
1/2 tsp	vanilla	2 mL
2/3 cup	oil	150 mL

Preheat oven to 350° F (180° C)
Muffin tin, paper-lined

1. In a bowl combine flour, baking powder, salt, sugar, cocoa powder and bran. Make a well in the center.

2. In another bowl combine eggs, milk, vanilla and oil; mix well. Pour into dry ingredients; stir just until moist and blended.

3. Spoon batter into prepared muffin tin. Bake in preheated oven for 18 to 20 minutes.

buttermilk bran muffins

1/3 cup	shortening	75 mL
1/2 cup	firmly packed brown sugar	125 mL
1	egg	1
1 cup	all-purpose flour	250 mL
1 tsp	baking powder	5 mL
1/2 tsp	baking soda	2 mL
1 tsp	salt	5 mL
3 cups	shredded bran cereal	750 mL
1 cup	buttermilk	250 mL

Preheat oven to 400° F (200° C)

12-cup muffin tin, greased or paper-lined

1. In a bowl cream together shortening, brown sugar and egg.

2. In another bowl sift together flour, baking powder, baking soda, salt and bran; mix well. Add to creamed mixture alternately with buttermilk; stir just until blended.

3. Spoon batter into prepared muffin tin, filling to top. Bake in preheated oven for about 20 minutes.

spiced carrot bran muffins

1 cup	all-bran cereal	250 mL
1 cup	buttermilk *or* sour milk	250 mL
1	egg, beaten	1
3/4 cup	finely shredded carrots (about 2 medium)	175 mL
3 tbsp	oil	45 mL
1 cup	all-purpose flour	250 mL
1/4 cup	packed brown sugar	50 mL
2 tsp	baking powder	10 mL
3/4 tsp	cinnamon *or* allspice	4 mL
1/2 tsp	baking soda	2 mL
1/2 tsp	salt	2 mL

Preheat oven to 400° F (200° C)

12-cup muffin tin, greased or paper-lined

1. In a bowl combine bran cereal and buttermilk. Let stand for about 5 minutes. Add egg, carrots and oil; mix well.

2. In another bowl combine flour, brown sugar, baking powder, cinnamon, baking soda, salt and bran mixture; stir just until blended.

3. Spoon batter into prepared muffin tin, dividing evenly. Bake in preheated oven for 15 to 20 minutes or until browned.

crunchy cheddar bran muffins

1 cup	all-bran cereal	250 mL
1 1/4 cups	buttermilk *or* sour milk	300 mL
1/4 cup	shortening	50 mL
1/3 cup	granulated sugar	75 mL
1	egg	1
1 1/2 cups	all-purpose flour	375 mL
1 1/2 tsp	baking powder	7 mL
1/2 tsp	salt	2 mL
1/4 tsp	baking soda	1 mL
1 cup	shredded sharp Cheddar cheese	250 mL

Preheat oven to 400° F (200° C)
12-cup muffin tin, greased

1. In a bowl cover bran with buttermilk. Let stand until softened.

2. In another bowl combine shortening and sugar; cream until light and fluffy. Beat in egg.

3. In another bowl sift together flour, baking powder, salt and baking soda. Add to creamed mixture alternately with bran mixture; stir in cheese.

4. Spoon batter into prepared muffin tin, filling three-quarters full. Bake in preheated oven for about 30 minutes.

chocolate chip bran muffins

1/2 cup	softened shortening	125 mL
2/3 cup	granulated sugar	150 mL
1	egg	1
1 tsp	vanilla	5 mL
1 1/2 cups	all-purpose flour	375 mL
1/2 tsp	baking soda	2 mL
3 tbsp	cocoa	45 mL
1/2 tsp	salt	2 mL
1 cup	buttermilk *or* sour milk	250 mL
1/2 cup	bran cereal	125 mL
1/2 cup	chocolate chips *or* carob	125 mL

Preheat oven to 350° F (180° C)
12-cup muffin tin, paper-lined

1. In a bowl cream together shortening, sugar, egg and vanilla.

2. In another bowl combine flour, baking soda, cocoa and salt. Add to creamed mixture alternately with buttermilk; stir just until blended. Add bran cereal and chocolate chips; stir well.

3. Spoon batter into prepared muffin tin, filling to top. Bake in preheated oven for about 25 minutes.

cream cheese bran muffins

Preheat oven to 375° F (190° C)
Muffin tin, greased or paper-lined

TOPPING

1	pkg (8 oz [250 g] softened cream cheese	1
1/4 cup	granulated sugar	50 mL
1	egg, beaten	1

1 1/4 cups	all-bran cereal	300 mL
1 cup	milk	250 mL
1/4 cup	vegetable oil	50 mL
1	egg, beaten	1
1 1/4 cups	all-purpose flour	300 mL
1/2 cup	granulated sugar	125 mL
1 tbsp	baking powder	15 mL
1/2 tsp	salt	2 mL
1/2 cup	raisins	125 mL

1. In a bowl combine cream cheese, sugar and egg; mix until blended well. Set aside.

2. In another bowl combine bran cereal and milk. Let stand for 2 minutes.

3. In another bowl combine oil and egg. Add to cereal mixture; mix well. Add flour, sugar, baking powder and salt; stir just until moist and blended. Fold in raisins.

4. Spoon batter into prepared muffin tin, filling three-quarters full. Drop 1 tbsp (15 mL) topping onto each muffin. Bake in preheated oven for 25 minutes.

all-bran sour cream muffins

Preheat oven to 425° F (220° C)
12-cup muffin tin, greased

1 cup	unsifted pastry flour	250 mL
3 tsp	baking powder	15 mL
1/2 tsp	baking soda	2 mL
1/2 tsp	salt	2 mL
1/4 cup	packed brown sugar	50 mL
3/4 cup	all-bran cereal	175 mL
2	egg whites	2
1/4 cup	dark molasses	50 mL
3/4 cup	sour cream	175 mL
3 tbsp	vegetable oil	45 mL

1. In a bowl sift together flour, baking powder, baking soda and salt. Add brown sugar and cereal; blend well.

2. In another bowl combine egg whites, molasses, sour cream and oil; beat well. Add to flour mixture; stir just until blended.

3. Spoon batter into prepared muffin tin, filling three-quarters full. Bake in preheated oven for 15 to 20 minutes.

double bran fig muffins

3/4 cup	whole wheat flour	175 mL
1/2 cup	natural bran	125 mL
1/2 cup	oat bran	125 mL
1/3 cup	wheat germ	75 mL
1/3 cup	packed brown sugar	75 mL
1 tsp	baking powder	5 mL
1/2 tsp	baking soda	2 mL
1/2 tsp	cinnamon	2 mL
1/4 tsp	salt	1 mL
1	egg	1
1 cup	buttermilk	250 mL
1/4 cup	vegetable oil	50 mL
1 cup	chopped figs	250 mL

Preheat oven to 375° F (190° C)
8-cup muffin tin, greased

1. In a bowl combine whole wheat flour, natural bran, oat bran, wheat germ, brown sugar, baking powder, baking soda, cinnamon and salt. Make a well in the center.

2. In another bowl whisk together egg, buttermilk and oil. Set aside 2 tbsp (25 mL) figs; add remaining figs to egg mixture. Pour into dry ingredients; stir just until blended. Do not overmix.

3. Spoon batter into prepared muffin tin; top with reserved figs. Bake in preheated oven for 20 to 25 minutes.

surprise-inside muffins

1 1/2 cups	all-purpose flour	375 mL
2 1/2 tsp	baking powder	12 mL
1/4 tsp	salt	1 mL
1 cup	oat bran	250 mL
1/2 cup	packed light brown sugar	125 mL
1 cup	milk	250 mL
1/3 cup	vegetable oil	75 mL
2	eggs, lightly beaten	2
1 tsp	vanilla	5 mL
1	pkg (3 oz [75 g]) cream cheese, cut into 12 pieces	1
3/4 cup	apricot-pineapple jam	175 mL

Preheat oven to 425° F (220° C)
12-cup muffin tin, greased

1. In a bowl sift together flour, baking powder and salt. Add oat bran and brown sugar. Set aside.

2. In another bowl combine milk, oil, eggs and vanilla. Add to dry ingredients; stir just until moist.

3. Spoon batter into prepared muffin tin, filling one-third full. Add 1 tbsp (15 mL) jam to each; top with 1 piece cream cheese. Spoon remaining batter over jam and cheese, dividing evenly. Bake in preheated oven for 14 to 16 minutes or until browned.

muffin stuff
These muffins are perfect for a special brunch or buffet.

honey bran muffins

1/2 cup	natural bran	125 mL
1/2 cup	toasted wheat germ	125 mL
1/2 cup	raisins	125 mL
1 cup	whole wheat flour	250 mL
2 1/2 tsp	baking powder	12 mL
1/2 tsp	baking soda	2 mL
1/2 tsp	salt	2 mL
1/4 tsp	cinnamon	1 mL
Pinch	nutmeg	Pinch
Pinch	allspice	Pinch
1	egg	1
3 tbsp	molasses	45 mL
1/4 cup	liquid honey	50 mL
1/3 cup	vegetable oil	75 mL
1 1/4 cups	milk	300 mL

Preheat oven to 400° F (200° C)
12-cup muffin tin, greased or paper-lined

1. In a bowl combine bran, wheat germ, raisins, flour, baking powder, baking soda, salt, cinnamon, nutmeg and allspice; mix well. Make a well in the center.

2. In another bowl whisk together egg, molasses, honey, oil and milk. Pour into dry ingredients; stir just until moistened (batter will be runny.)

3. Spoon batter into prepared muffin tin, filling three-quarters full. Bake in preheated oven for about 15 minutes.

sour cream-raisin muffins

1	egg	1
1 cup	sour cream	250 mL
1/2 cup	milk	125 mL
1/2 cup	raisins	125 mL
1 3/4 cups	all-purpose flour	425 mL
2 tbsp	granulated sugar	25 mL
1 tsp	baking powder	5 mL
1/2 tsp	baking soda	2 mL
1/2 tsp	salt	2 mL
1 tsp	nutmeg	5 mL

Preheat oven to 400° F (200° C)
12-cup muffin tin, greased or paper-lined

1. In a bowl combine egg, sour cream and milk; beat well. Add raisins.

2. In another bowl sift together flour, sugar, baking powder, baking soda, salt and nutmeg. Add egg mixture; stir just until moist and blended. Do not overmix.

3. Spoon batter into prepared muffin tin, filling three-quarters full. Bake in preheated oven for 15 to 20 minutes.

prune bran muffins

1 1/2 cups	all-purpose flour	375 mL
1/2 cup	granulated sugar	125 mL
1 tbsp	baking powder	15 mL
1 tsp	salt	5 mL
1 1/2 cups	whole bran cereal	375 mL
1 cup	milk	250 mL
1/2 cup	chopped pitted prunes	125 mL
1	egg	1
1/3 cup	oil	75 mL

Preheat oven to 400° F (200° C)
12-cup muffin tin, greased

1. In a bowl combine flour, sugar, baking powder and salt.

2. In another bowl combine cereal, milk and prunes. Let stand for 2 minutes. Add egg and oil; beat well. Add to flour mixture; stir just until moist and blended. Do not overmix.

3. Spoon batter into prepared muffin tin, filling two-thirds or three-quarters full. Bake in preheated oven for 15 to 20 minutes or until golden brown.

bran oat muffins

2	eggs, beaten	2
1 cup	brown sugar	250 mL
3/4 cup	oil	175 mL
2 cups	milk	500 mL
1/3 cup	bran	75 mL
1/3 cup	oatmeal	75 mL
1/3 cup	wheat germ	75 mL
1 tsp	baking soda	5 mL
2 tsp	baking powder	10 mL
1 tsp	salt	5 mL
2 cups	all-purpose flour	500 mL
1 cup	raisins or dates	250 mL
1/4 cup	walnuts (optional)	50 mL
1 tsp	cinnamon	5 mL
1 tsp	vanilla	5 mL

Preheat oven to 350° F (180° C)
Muffin tin, greased or paper-lined

1. In a bowl combine eggs, sugar, oil and milk; whisk until well blended. Add bran, oatmeal, wheat germ, baking soda, baking powder, salt, flour, raisins, walnuts, cinnamon and vanilla. Stir just until moist and blended.

2. Spoon batter into prepared muffin tin. Bake in preheated oven for 15 to 20 minutes.

tangerine bran muffins

1 cup	all-bran cereal	250 mL
3/4 cup	milk	175 mL
2 tsp	grated tangerine zest	10 mL
1/3 cup	freshly squeezed tangerine juice	75 mL
1	egg, beaten	1
1/4 cup	oil	50 mL
1 1/4 cups	all-purpose flour	300 mL
1/4 cup	granulated sugar	50 mL
3 tsp	baking powder	15 mL
1/4 tsp	baking soda	1 mL
1/4 tsp	salt	1 mL
1	tangerine, divided into sections	1

Preheat oven to 400° F (200° C)
Muffin tin, greased or paper-lined

1. In a bowl combine bran cereal, milk, zest, juice, egg and oil; blend well.

2. In another bowl sift together flour, sugar, baking powder, baking soda and salt. Add to bran mixture; stir just until moist and blended.

3. Spoon batter into prepared muffin tin, filling three-quarters full. Top each with an orange section. Bake in preheated oven for 20 to 25 minutes.

cereal breakfast muffins

2 cups	all-purpose flour	500 mL
1/2 cup	granulated sugar or brown sugar	125 mL
1 tbsp	baking powder	15 mL
1 tsp	cinnamon	5 mL
1/4 tsp	nutmeg	1 mL
1/2 tsp	salt	2 mL
1 cup	milk	250 mL
1	egg	1
1 tsp	vanilla	5 mL
1/3 cup	vegetable oil	75 mL
1	medium apple or pear, peeled and coarsely chopped	1
1/2 cup	raisins	125 mL
2 cups	dry cereal	500 mL

Preheat oven to 375° F (190° C)
12-cup muffin tin, paper-lined

1. In a bowl combine flour, sugar, baking powder, cinnamon, nutmeg and salt. Make a well in the center.

2. In another bowl beat together milk, egg, vanilla and oil. Add apple, raisins and cereal. Pour into dry ingredients; stir just until moistened.

3. Spoon batter into prepared muffin tin. Bake in preheated oven for 25 to 30 minutes.

spicy bran-sweet potato muffins

Preheat oven to 350° F (180° C)
16-cup muffin tin, greased

CRUMB TOPPING

3/4 cup	crushed bran flakes cereal	175 mL
2 tbsp	butter or margarine, melted	25 mL
2 tbsp	light brown sugar	25 mL
1 cup	vegetable oil	250 mL
3/4 cup	firmly packed light brown sugar	175 mL
2	eggs	2
1 tsp	vanilla	5 mL
1/2 cup	crushed bran flakes cereal	125 mL
1 cup	all-purpose flour	250 mL
1 1/2 tsp	baking soda	7 mL
1/2 tsp	salt	2 mL
1/2 tsp	cinnamon	2 mL
1/4 tsp	ginger	1 mL
1/8 tsp	cloves	0.5 mL
1/8 tsp	allspice	0.5 mL
1 tsp	grated orange zest	5 mL
1 1/2 cups	pared shredded sweet potato	375 mL
1 cup	chopped almonds	250 mL

1. In a bowl combine cereal, butter and sugar. Set aside.

2. In another bowl combine oil, brown sugar, eggs and vanilla; beat on high for 2 minutes.

3. In another bowl combine crushed cereal, flour, baking soda, salt, cinnamon, ginger, cloves and allspice; mix well. Add orange zest. Add to oil mixture; stir just until blended. Fold in sweet potato and almonds.

4. Spoon batter into prepared muffin tin, filling two-thirds full. Sprinkle topping evenly over tops. Bake in preheated oven for about 20 minutes.

upside-down honey bran muffins

1 cup	honey	250 mL
1/2 cup	water	125 mL
1/2 cup	walnuts	125 mL
1 cup	whole wheat flour	250 mL
1 cup	natural bran	250 mL
1 cup	bran cereal	250 mL
1 tsp	baking soda	5 mL
3 tsp	baking powder	15 mL
1 tsp	salt	5 mL
2	eggs	2
1 cup	sour cream	250 mL
1 cup	raisins	250 mL

Preheat oven to 350° F (180° C)
18-cup muffin tin, greased

1. In a saucepan over low heat, combine honey and water; gently warm until blended.

2. Spoon 1 tbsp (15 mL) walnuts into each muffin cup; cover with 1 tbsp (15 mL) warm honey mixture.

3. In a bowl combine flour, natural bran, bran cereal, baking soda, baking powder and salt.

4. In another bowl whisk together eggs and sour cream; fold in raisins. Add remaining warm honey mixture. Add to flour mixture; stir quickly just until moist and blended.

5. Spoon batter into muffin tin, filling to top. Bake in preheated oven for about 25 minutes. Cool slightly; invert pan over a large plate or tray so that honey mixture is now a topping.

lemon yogurt-cranberry muffins

2/3 cup	honey	150 mL
1/3 cup	oil	75 mL
4	eggs	4
1 1/2 tsp	lemon extract	7 mL
1 3/4 cups	all-purpose flour	425 mL
3/4 cup	whole wheat flour	175 mL
2 1/2 tsp	baking powder	12 mL
1 cup	lemon yogurt	250 mL
1 cup	coarsely chopped cranberries	250 mL
1 tbsp	grated lemon zest	15 mL

Preheat oven to 400° F (200° C)
Muffin tin, greased or paper-lined

1. In a bowl beat together honey and oil until creamy. Add eggs and lemon extract; blend well.

2. In another bowl combine all-purpose flour, whole wheat flour and baking powder. Add to egg mixture alternately with yogurt, beginning and ending with flour mixture. Fold in cranberries and lemon zest. Do not overmix.

3. Spoon batter into prepared muffin tin, filling to top. Bake in preheated oven for 15 to 20 minutes.

applesauce cheese muffins

2 cups	whole wheat flour	500 mL
1/4 cup	wheat germ	50 mL
2 tbsp	granulated sugar	25 mL
1 tbsp	baking powder	15 mL
1/2 tsp	baking soda	2 mL
1/4 tsp	salt	1 mL
1/4 cup	softened butter or margarine	50 mL
1 1/2 cups	grated Cheddar cheese	375 mL
2	eggs, lightly beaten	2
3/4 cup	milk	175 mL
3/4 cup	applesauce	175 mL

Preheat oven to 400° F (200° C)
12-cup muffin tin, greased

1. In a bowl combine flour, wheat germ, sugar, baking powder, baking soda and salt. Cut in butter with a pastry blender until mixture is crumbly. Add cheese.

2. In another bowl, combine remaining ingredients. Pour all at once into dry ingredients and stir just until blended.

3. Spoon batter into prepared muffin tin, filling three-quarters full. Bake in preheated oven for 18 to 20 minutes.

beer and cheese muffins

2 cups	all-purpose flour	500 mL
2 tbsp	granulated sugar	25 mL
1 tsp	baking powder	5 mL
1/4 tsp	dry mustard	1 mL
1 cup	beer	250 mL
1/4 cup	oil	50 mL
1	egg, beaten	1
1 1/4 cups	grated sharp Cheddar cheese	300 mL

Preheat oven to 400° F (200° C)
Muffin tin, greased or paper-lined

1. In a bowl combine flour, sugar, baking powder and mustard. Make a well in the center.

2. In another bowl combine beer, oil, egg and cheese. Add to dry ingredients; stir just until blended.

3. Spoon batter into prepared muffin tin, filling three-quarters full. Bake in preheated oven for 20 to 25 minutes.

cheddar cheese apple muffins

1	egg	1
1 1/4 cups	milk	300 mL
1/4 cup	melted margarine	50 mL
2 1/2 cups	all-purpose flour	625 mL
1/4 cup	granulated sugar	50 mL
1 tbsp	baking powder	15 mL
1 tsp	salt	5 mL
1 cup	grated unpeeled apple	250 mL
1 1/4 cups	grated old Cheddar cheese	300 mL

Preheat oven to 400° F (200° C)

12-cup muffin tin, greased or paper-lined

1. In a bowl beat egg lightly with a fork. Add milk and margarine; stir well.

2. In a bowl combine flour, sugar, baking powder and salt. Add egg mixture; stir just until blended. Fold in apple and 1 cup (250 mL) cheese.

3. Spoon batter into prepared muffin tin, dividing equally. Sprinkle with remaining cheese. Bake in preheated oven for about 20 minutes or until golden brown.

cheese and mustard muffins

2 tbsp	minced green onions	25 mL
2 tbsp	minced red bell pepper	25 mL
4 tbsp	unsalted butter	50 mL
1 cup	all-purpose flour	250 mL
1 cup	whole wheat pastry flour	250 mL
2 1/2 tsp	baking powder	12 mL
1/2 tsp	salt	2 mL
2	eggs	2
1 cup	milk	250 mL
2 tbsp	Dijon mustard	25 mL
1 tbsp	granulated sugar	15 mL
1 cup	grated Cheddar cheese	250 mL

Preheat oven to 375° F (190° C)

Muffin tin, greased

1. In a saucepan over medium-high heat, combine onions, pepper and butter. Sauté until soft; set aside.

2. In a bowl combine all-purpose flour, whole wheat flour, baking powder and salt; mix well.

3. In another bowl combine eggs, milk, mustard and sugar; whisk well. Stir in cheese. Add onion mixture and flour mixture; stir just until moist and blended.

4. Spoon batter into prepared muffin tin, dividing evenly. Bake in preheated oven for 20 to 25 minutes.

cheesy tuna 'n' rice muffins

2 cups	cooked rice	500 mL
1 cup	shredded Cheddar cheese	250 mL
1	can (7 1/2 oz [213 g]) drained flaked tuna	1
3/4 cup	black olives, sliced into thirds	175 mL
1 tbsp	chopped onion	15 mL
1 tbsp	parsley flakes	15 mL
1 tsp	seasoned salt	5 mL
2	eggs, beaten	2
2 tbsp	milk	25 mL

TANGY BUTTER SAUCE

1/4 cup	melted butter or margarine	50 mL
1 tbsp	lemon juice	15 mL
1/2 tsp	seasoned salt	2 mL
1/2 tsp	parsley flakes	2 mL

Preheat oven to 375° F (190° C)
6-cup muffin tin, greased

1. In a bowl combine rice, cheese, tuna, olives, onion, parsley and salt. Add eggs and milk; mix thoroughly.

2. Spoon batter into prepared muffin tin, dividing evenly. Bake in preheated oven for 15 minutes or until lightly browned.

3. Meanwhile, in a bowl combine butter, lemon juice, salt and parsley; mix well. Spoon over warm muffins.

potato cheese muffins

2 cups	all-purpose flour	500 mL
1/2 cup	granulated sugar	125 mL
4 tsp	baking powder	20 mL
1 tsp	salt	5 mL
2	eggs	2
1 1/2 cups	milk	375 mL
1/2 cup	cooled mashed potatoes	125 mL
1/2 cup	shredded Cheddar cheese	125 mL
1/3 cup	melted shortening	75 mL

Preheat oven to 400° F (200° C)
Muffin tin, greased or paper-lined

1. In a bowl combine flour, sugar, baking powder and salt. Make a well in the center.

2. In another bowl beat eggs well. Add milk, potatoes, cheese and shortening; mix well. Add to flour mixture, stirring just until moistened.

3. Spoon batter into prepared muffin tin, dividing evenly. Bake in preheated oven for 25 minutes or until lightly browned.

muffin stuff

A great way to use today's leftover potatoes for tomorrow's lunch.

cheesy mushroom muffins

3 tbsp	butter *or* margarine	45 mL
3 cups	finely chopped mushrooms	750 mL
1 cup	whole wheat flour	250 mL
1 cup	all-purpose flour	250 mL
3 tsp	baking powder	15 mL
2 tsp	granulated sugar	10 mL
1/2 tsp	salt	2 mL
1 cup	grated old Cheddar cheese	250 mL
3/4 cup	milk	175 mL
2	eggs	2

Preheat oven to 375° F (190° C)
Muffin tin, greased

1. In a skillet heat butter over medium-high heat. Add mushrooms; cook quickly until golden brown and no moisture is left.

2. In a bowl sift together whole wheat flour, all-purpose flour, baking powder, sugar and salt. Add cheese; toss to coat well.

3. In another bowl beat together milk and eggs. Add to flour mixture; mix well. Add mushrooms.

4. Spoon batter into prepared muffin tin, dividing evenly. Bake in preheated oven for 30 minutes.

mashed potato muffins

10	medium-sized potatoes	10
1 tsp	salt	5 mL
1/2 tsp	pepper	2 mL
2 tbsp	oil	25 mL
4	eggs, beaten	4
2	onions, chopped	2

Preheat oven to 400° F (200° C)
2 12-cup muffin tins, greased

1. In a saucepan of boiling water, cook potatoes until soft. In a bowl combine cooked potatoes, salt, pepper and oil; mash until smooth. Add eggs; mix well.

2. In a frying pan over medium-high heat, cook onions for about 2 minutes. Add to potato mixture; stir well.

3. In preheated oven heat prepared muffin tin. Spoon batter into hot tin. Bake in preheated oven for 30 to 40 minutes.

cornmeal bacon muffins

6	bacon slices, chopped	6
1 1/2 cups	all-purpose flour	375 mL
1/2 cup	cornmeal	125 mL
1 tbsp	baking powder	15 mL
1/2 tsp	salt	2 mL
Pinch	cayenne red pepper (optional)	Pinch
1 1/4 cups	coarsely grated Cheddar cheese	300 mL
1	egg	1
1 cup	milk	250 mL
1/4 cup	melted butter or margarine	50 mL

TOPPING

1/3 cup	coarsely grated Cheddar cheese	75 mL

Preheat oven to 425° F (220° C)
12-cup muffin tin, greased or paper-lined

1. In a skillet over medium-high heat, cook bacon until crisp; drain. Set aside to cool.

2. In a bowl combine flour, cornmeal, baking powder, salt, cayenne (if desired), Cheddar cheese and bacon.

3. In another bowl whisk egg; add milk and melted butter. Add to flour mixture; stir just until moist and blended.

4. Spoon batter into prepared muffin tin, filling three-quarters full. Sprinkle with cheese topping. Bake in preheated oven for 20 minutes or until golden brown.

tangy cottage cheese muffins

1	egg, slightly beaten	1
1/4 cup	vegetable oil	50 mL
1/2 cup	milk	125 mL
1 cup	cottage cheese	250 mL
2 tbsp	chopped green onions	25 mL
2 tsp	finely chopped fresh dill	10 mL
1/2 tsp	Worcestershire sauce	2 mL
2 cups	all-purpose flour	500 mL
1 tbsp	baking powder	15 mL
1/2 tsp	seasoned salt	2 mL

Preheat oven to 400° F (200° C)
12-cup muffin tin, greased

1. In a bowl combine egg, oil, milk, cheese, onions, dill and Worcestershire sauce; stir well. Add flour, baking powder and salt; stir just until moist and blended.

2. Spoon batter into prepared muffin tin, dividing evenly. Bake in preheated oven for 20 minutes.

cheese danish muffins

1	pkg (4 oz [125 g]) softened cream cheese	1
2 tbsp	granulated sugar	25 mL
1 tbsp	lemon juice	15 mL
1	egg	1
1 1/4 cups	milk	300 mL
1/2 cup	melted margarine	125 mL
1 tsp	grated lemon zest	5 mL
2 1/2 cups	all-purpose flour	625 mL
1/2 cup	granulated sugar	125 mL
3 1/2 tsp	baking powder	17 mL
1 tsp	salt	5 mL

Preheat oven to 400° F (200° C)
12-cup muffin tin, greased or paper-lined

1. In a bowl cream together cheese, sugar and lemon juice. Set aside.

2. In another bowl beat egg lightly with a fork; add milk, margarine and zest.

3. In another bowl combine flour, sugar, baking powder and salt. Add egg mixture; stir just until blended.

4. Spoon batter into prepared muffin tin, filling half full. Place 1 tbsp (15 mL) cheese mixture over each; top with remaining batter. Bake in preheated oven for 20 minutes.

cheese and rice muffins

8 oz	dry cottage cheese	250 g
3/4 cup	cooked rice	175 mL
1 tbsp	butter or margarine, melted	15 mL
1 tbsp	oil	15 mL
3 tbsp	granulated sugar	45 mL
3 tbsp	sour cream	45 mL
3	eggs, beaten	3
3/4 cup	all-purpose flour	175 mL
2 tsp	baking powder	10 mL

Preheat oven to 425° F (220° C)
12-cup muffin tin, greased

1. In a bowl combine cottage cheese, rice, butter, oil, sugar, sour cream, eggs, flour and baking powder.

2. Place empty prepared muffin tin in preheated oven; heat until sizzling. Remove from oven. Spoon batter into hot tin, dividing evenly. Bake in preheated oven for 20 to 25 minutes.

nutritious health muffins

4	eggs	4
1 1/2 cups	canola oil	375 mL
2 1/2 cups	brown sugar	625 mL
1 tbsp	salt	15 mL
2 1/2 cups	milk	625 mL
1 tbsp	baking soda	15 mL
3 tbsp	molasses	45 mL
1/2 cup	applesauce	125 mL
3/4 cup	walnut pieces *or* 1 apple, peeled and grated	175 mL
1 cup	chopped dates	250 mL
1 cup	raisins	250 mL
5 1/2 cups	whole wheat flour	1.375 L

Preheat oven to 375° F (190° C)

Muffin tin, greased or paper-lined

1. In a bowl beat together eggs and oil. Add brown sugar; mix well. Gradually add salt, milk, baking soda, molasses, applesauce, walnut pieces, dates, raisins and whole wheat flour; stir just until blended.

2. Spoon batter into prepared muffin tins, dividing evenly (makes 30 to 36 muffins). Bake in preheated oven for about 25 minutes.

fresh herb muffins

1 1/2 cups	all-purpose flour	375 mL
1 tbsp	granulated sugar	15 mL
1 1/2 tsp	baking powder	7 mL
1/2 tsp	baking soda	2 mL
Pinch	salt	Pinch
1 tsp	garlic powder	5 mL
1/3 cup	grated Parmesan cheese	75 mL
1/2 cup	finely chopped fresh herbs (oregano or basil)	125 mL
1	egg	1
2 tbsp	butter, melted	25 mL
1 1/4 cups	buttermilk	300 mL

Preheat oven to 400° F (200° C)

12-cup muffin tin, greased or paper-lined

1. In a bowl sift together flour, sugar, baking powder, baking soda, salt and garlic powder. Add cheese and herbs; stir well.

2. In another bowl beat egg lightly with a fork; add butter and buttermilk. Add to dry ingredients; mix quickly just until moistened.

3. Spoon batter into prepared muffin tin, filling three-quarters full. Bake in preheated oven for 15 to 20 minutes.

double good oat bran muffins

Preheat oven to 400° F (200° C)
18-cup muffin tin, greased

1 cup	quick oats	250 mL
1 cup	all-purpose flour	250 mL
1 cup	oat bran	250 mL
1 tsp	baking soda	5 mL
1 tbsp	baking powder	15 mL
1/2 tsp	salt	2 mL
1/2 cup	chopped pecans	125 mL
1/2 cup	chopped almonds	125 mL
1 cup	plain yogurt	250 mL
1 cup	buttermilk	250 mL
1	egg	1
1 tsp	vanilla	5 mL
4 tbsp	butter or margarine, melted *or* oil	50 mL
1/2 cup	dark brown sugar	125 mL

1. In a bowl combine oats, flour, oat bran, baking soda, baking powder, salt, pecans and almonds; mix well.

2. In another bowl whisk together yogurt, buttermilk, egg, vanilla, butter and brown sugar. Add to dry ingredients; stir just until blended.

3. Spoon batter into prepared muffin tin, dividing evenly. Bake in preheated oven for 18 to 20 minutes.

banana-raisin oat bran muffins

Preheat oven to 400° F (200° C)
12-cup muffin tin, paper-lined

1 cup	whole wheat flour	250 mL
1 tsp	baking powder	5 mL
1 tsp	baking soda	5 mL
1 cup	oat bran	250 mL
1/2 cup	raisins	125 mL
1	egg, lightly beaten	1
1/4 cup	oil	50 mL
1/2 cup	granulated sugar	125 mL
1 cup	mashed bananas	250 mL
1 tsp	vanilla	5 mL

1. In a bowl combine flour, baking powder, baking soda, oat bran and raisins.

2. In another bowl combine egg, oil, sugar, bananas and vanilla. Add to flour mixture; stir just until blended.

3. Spoon batter into prepared muffin tin, dividing evenly. Bake in preheated oven for 20 to 25 minutes.

carrot chipit oat bran muffins

1 1/4 cups	whole wheat flour	300 mL
1 cup	oat bran	250 mL
1/2 cup	firmly packed brown sugar	125 mL
1 tsp	baking soda	5 mL
1 cup	butterscotch chips *or* chocolate chips	250 mL
1 cup	grated carrots	250 mL
3/4 cup	plain yogurt	175 mL
1/2 cup	chopped pecans	125 mL
1/2 cup	melted butter	125 mL
1 1/2 tsp	grated orange zest	7 mL
2	eggs	2

Preheat oven to 400° F (200° C)
12-cup muffin tin, greased or paper-lined

1. In a bowl combine flour, bran, brown sugar, baking soda and butterscotch chips; mix well.

2. In another bowl combine carrots, yogurt, pecans, butter, zest and eggs. Add to dry ingredients; stir just until blended.

3. Spoon batter into prepared muffin tin, filling three-quarters full. Bake in preheated oven for 25 to 30 minutes.

oat bran fruit muffins

2 1/4 cups	oat bran	550 mL
1/2 cup	packaged mixed dried diced fruit	125 mL
1 tsp	cinnamon	5 mL
1 tsp	baking powder	5 mL
1/2 tsp	baking soda	2 mL
1/4 tsp	salt	1 mL
2	egg whites	2
1 cup	unsweetened applesauce	250 mL
1/2 cup	packed brown sugar	125 mL
1/2 cup	buttermilk *or* plain yogurt	125 mL
2 tbsp	vegetable oil	25 mL

Preheat oven to 350° F (180° C)
Muffin tin, greased

1. In a bowl combine oat bran, dried fruit, cinnamon, baking powder, baking soda and salt.

2. In another bowl whisk together egg whites, applesauce, brown sugar, buttermilk and oil. Add to dry ingredients; stir just until blended.

3. Spoon batter into prepared muffin tin, filling three-quarters full. Bake in preheated oven for 30 to 35 minutes.

honey-nut oat bran muffins

2 cups	oat bran cereal	500 mL
1/3 cup	all-purpose flour	75 mL
2 tbsp	packed brown sugar	25 mL
1/4 cup	chopped nuts	50 mL
1/4 cup	raisins	50 mL
1 tbsp	baking powder	15 mL
1/2 tsp	salt	2 mL
1/4 tsp	cinnamon	1 mL
1 cup	milk	250 mL
2	eggs, beaten	2
1/3 cup	honey *or* molasses	75 mL
2 tbsp	vegetable oil	25 mL

Preheat oven to 425° F (220° C)
Muffin tin, greased or paper-lined

1. In a bowl combine cereal, flour, brown sugar, nuts, raisins, baking powder, salt and cinnamon. Make a well in the center. Add milk, eggs, honey and oil; stir just until moist and blended.

2. Spoon batter into prepared muffin tin, filling three-quarters full. Bake in preheated oven for 15 to 20 minutes or until golden brown.

orange oat bran muffins

1 cup	oat bran	250 mL
1 cup	whole wheat flour	250 mL
3/4 cup	all-purpose flour	175 mL
1/2 cup	quick-cooking oats	125 mL
1 tbsp	baking powder	15 mL
1/2 tsp	cinnamon	2 mL
1/4 tsp	salt	1 mL
2	eggs, lightly beaten	2
1 cup	orange juice	250 mL
2 tsp	grated orange zest	10 mL
1/2 cup	honey	125 mL
1/3 cup	oil	75 mL
1/4 cup	skim milk	50 mL

Preheat oven to 400° F (200° C)
12-cup muffin tin, lightly greased

1. In a bowl combine oat bran, whole wheat flour, all-purpose flour, oats, baking powder, cinnamon and salt; blend well. Make a well in the center.

2. In another bowl combine eggs, juice, zest, honey, oil and milk; blend well. Add to dry ingredients; stir just until blended.

3. Spoon batter into prepared muffin tin, filling to top. Bake in preheated oven for 15 to 20 minutes.

vegetable oat bran muffins

4 cups	oat bran	1 L
1 cup	all-purpose flour	250 mL
2 tbsp	baking powder	25 mL
2 tbsp	cornstarch	25 mL
1/2 tsp	salt	2 mL
2 tbsp	cinnamon	25 mL
1/2 tsp	nutmeg	2 mL
2 cups	skim milk	500 mL
1/2 cup	brown sugar	125 mL
4 tbsp	vegetable oil	60 mL
2	eggs	2
1 tbsp	vanilla	15 mL
2 tbsp	corn syrup	25 mL
2 cups	grated carrots, zucchini or apple *or* mashed banana *or* 1 can (14 oz [398 mL]) pumpkin	500 mL
1 1/2.cups	raisins *or* currants *or* chopped dates (or a mixture)	375 mL

Preheat oven to 425° F (220° C)
Muffin tin, greased

1. In a bowl combine oat bran, flour, baking powder, cornstarch, salt, cinnamon and nutmeg. Make a well in the center.

2. In another bowl, combine milk, brown sugar, oil, eggs, vanilla, corn syrup, carrots and raisins; blend well. Add to dry ingredients; stir just until moistened.

3. Spoon batter into prepared muffin tin, dividing evenly. Bake in preheated oven for 15 to 20 minutes.

grandma's old-fashioned oatmeal muffins

Preheat oven to 425° F (220° C)
Muffin tin, greased or paper-lined

3/4 cup	regular rolled oats	175 mL
3/4 cup + 2 tbsp	all-purpose flour	175 mL + 25 mL
2 tbsp	firmly packed light brown sugar	25 mL
1 1/2 tsp	baking powder	7 mL
1/2 tsp	baking soda	2 mL
1/2 tsp	salt	2 mL
1 tsp	cinnamon	5 mL
1/4 cup	butter *or* margarine	50 mL
1	egg	1
3/4 cup	buttermilk	175 mL
TOPPING		
1/3 cup	granulated sugar	75 mL
1 1/2 tsp	cinnamon	7 mL
1 tbsp	margarine, melted	15 mL

1. In a bowl combine oats, flour, brown sugar, baking powder, baking soda, salt and cinnamon; mix well. Cut in butter; mix until crumbly.

2. In another bowl beat together egg and buttermilk. Pour into dry ingredients; stir just until blended.

3. In another bowl, combine sugar, cinnamon and margarine; mix well.

4. Spoon batter into prepared muffin tin, filling two-thirds full. Sprinkle with topping. Bake in preheated oven for 15 to 20 minutes.

maple oat muffins

Preheat oven to 400° F (200° C)
Muffin tin, paper-lined

1 cup	maple oats	250 mL
1 cup	sour cream	250 mL
1 cup	all-purpose flour	250 mL
1/2 cup	brown sugar	125 mL
1 tsp	baking powder	5 mL
1/2 tsp	baking soda	2 mL
1/2 tsp	salt	2 mL
1	egg, beaten	1
1/4 cup	vegetable oil	50 mL

1. In a bowl combine oats and sour cream. Set aside.

2. In another bowl combine flour, brown sugar, baking powder, baking soda and salt.

3. Add egg and oil to oat mixture; blend well. Add dry ingredients; mix together quickly just until moist. Do not overmix (batter will be lumpy.)

4. Spoon batter into prepared muffin tin, filling two-thirds full. Bake in preheated oven for 15 to 20 minutes.

scrumptious blueberry oat muffins

1 cup	oats	250 mL
1 cup	buttermilk	250 mL
1	egg, beaten	1
1/4 cup	butter or margarine, melted	50 mL
1 cup	all-purpose flour	250 mL
1 tsp	baking powder	5 mL
1/2 tsp	baking soda	2 mL
1/2 tsp	salt	2 mL
3/4 cup	lightly packed brown sugar	175 mL
1 cup	fresh blueberries or frozen blueberries, thawed and drained	250 mL

Preheat oven to 400° F (200° C)

12-cup muffin tin, greased

1. In a bowl combine oats and buttermilk; mix well. Let stand for 5 to 10 minutes. Add egg and butter; blend well.

2. In another bowl combine flour, baking powder, baking soda, salt and brown sugar. Add oat mixture; stir just until moist and blended. Fold in blueberries.

3. Spoon batter into prepared muffin tin, dividing evenly. Bake in preheated oven for 15 to 20 minutes.

buttermilk oatmeal muffins

1 cup	quick-cooking oats	250 mL
1 cup	buttermilk	250 mL
1	egg, beaten	1
1/2 cup	brown sugar	125 mL
1/4 cup	melted shortening, cooled or vegetable oil	50 mL
1/2 cup	all-purpose flour	125 mL
1/2 cup	whole wheat pastry flour	125 mL
1 1/2 tsp	baking powder	7 mL
1/2 tsp	baking soda	2 mL
1/2 tsp	salt	2 mL

Preheat oven to 400° F (200° C)

12-cup muffin tin, greased

1. In a bowl combine oats and buttermilk. Let stand for 50 to 60 minutes.

2. In another bowl combine egg, brown sugar and shortening; mix well. Add to oat mixture; blend well. Add all-purpose flour, whole wheat flour, baking powder, baking soda and salt; stir just until moist and blended.

3. Spoon batter into prepared muffin tin, dividing evenly. Bake in preheated oven for 15 to 20 minutes or until browned.

chocolate chip oatmeal muffins

1 cup	old-fashioned oats	250 mL
2 cups	buttermilk	500 mL
2	lightly beaten eggs	2
1 2/3 cups	whole wheat flour	410 mL
1 tsp	baking soda	5 mL
1 tsp	salt	5 mL
2 tbsp	vegetable oil	25 mL
1 cup	chocolate chips	250 mL

Muffin tin, greased or paper-lined

1. In a bowl combine oats and buttermilk. Cover; refrigerate overnight. The next day, add beaten eggs; whisk well.

2. In another bowl sift together flour, baking soda, salt and oil. Add to oat mixture; stir just until blended. Fold in chocolate chips.

3. Spoon batter into prepared muffin tin, filling to the top. Bake at 400° F (200° C) for 15 to 20 minutes.

garden oatmeal muffins

1 1/2 cups	quick-cooking oats	375 mL
1 1/2 cups	milk	375 mL
1	egg	1
1/2 cup	margarine, melted	125 mL
1 cup	all-purpose flour	250 mL
1 cup	whole wheat flour	250 mL
1/2 cup	firmly packed brown sugar	125 mL
3 1/2 tsp	baking powder	17 mL
1 tsp	salt	5 mL
1 tsp	cinnamon	5 mL
1/2 tsp	nutmeg	2 mL
1 cup	grated carrots	250 mL
1 cup	grated zucchini	250 mL

Preheat oven to 400° F (200° C)
12-cup muffin tin, greased or paper-lined

1. In a bowl cover oats with milk. Let stand for 5 minutes. Add egg and margarine; blend well.

2. In another bowl combine all-purpose flour, whole wheat flour, brown sugar, baking powder, salt, cinnamon and nutmeg; blend well. Add oat mixture; stir just until moist. Fold in carrots and zucchini.

3. Spoon batter into prepared muffin tin, filling to top. Bake in preheated oven for about 20 minutes.

pineapple oatmeal muffins

1	can (8 oz [250 g]) crushed pineapple, not drained	1
1 cup	sour cream	250 mL
1	egg	1
1/4 cup	butter or margarine, melted	50 mL
1 1/2 cups	all-purpose flour	375 mL
1 cup	old-fashioned oats	250 mL
1/2 cup	granulated sugar	125 mL
1 tbsp	baking powder	15 mL
1 tsp	cinnamon	5 mL
1/2 tsp	nutmeg	2 mL
1/2 tsp	salt	2 mL
1 cup	raisins (optional)	250 mL

Preheat oven to 350° F (180° C)
12-cup muffin tin, greased or paper-lined

1. In a bowl combine pineapple, sour cream, egg and butter; blend well.

2. In another bowl combine flour, oats, sugar, baking powder, cinnamon, nutmeg, salt and raisins. Add to pineapple mixture; stir just until moist.

3. Spoon batter into prepared muffin tin, dividing evenly. Bake in preheated oven for 30 to 35 minutes or until lightly browned.

whole wheat oatmeal muffins

1/2 cup	all-purpose flour	125 mL
1/2 cup	whole wheat flour	125 mL
1 cup	old-fashioned oats	250 mL
2 tsp	baking powder	10 mL
1/2 tsp	salt	2 mL
2	eggs	2
3/4 cup	packed brown sugar	175 mL
3/4 cup	milk	175 mL
1/4 cup	butter or margarine, melted	50 mL
1 tsp	vanilla	5 mL

Preheat oven to 400° F (200° C)
Muffin tin, greased

1. In a bowl combine all-purpose flour, whole wheat flour, oats, baking powder and salt; blend well.

2. In another bowl whisk together eggs, brown sugar, milk, butter and vanilla. Add to dry mixture; stir just until blended.

3. Spoon batter into prepared muffin tin, filling three-quarters full. Bake in preheated oven for 15 to 20 minutes.

banana wheat germ muffins

2	small ripe bananas *or* 1 large banana, mashed	2
1/2 cup	granulated sugar *or* brown sugar	125 mL
1/3 cup	vegetable oil	75 mL
1	egg	1
1 tsp	vanilla	5 mL
1/2 cup	wheat germ	125 mL
1 1/2 cups	all-purpose flour	375 mL
1 tsp	baking powder	5 mL
1 tsp	baking soda	5 mL
1/2 cup	milk	125 mL

Preheat oven to 375° F (190° C)

12-cup muffin tin, greased or paper-lined

1. In a bowl combine bananas, sugar, oil, egg and vanilla; beat until smooth. Add wheat germ; blend well.

2. In another bowl sift together flour, baking powder and baking soda. Add to banana mixture alternately with milk; stir just until blended.

3. Spoon batter into prepared muffin tin, filling to top. Bake in preheated oven for 20 to 25 minutes.

wheat germ oat muffins

1/2 cup	wheat germ	125 mL
1/2 cup	quick-cooking oats	125 mL
1 cup	all-purpose flour	250 mL
3 tsp	baking powder	15 mL
1/2 tsp	salt	2 mL
3/4 tsp	cinnamon	4 mL
Pinch	nutmeg	Pinch
1/2 cup	brown sugar	125 mL
1/3 cup	shortening	75 mL
1	egg, slightly beaten	1
1 cup	milk	250 mL
1 tsp	vanilla	5 mL

Preheat oven to 425° F (220° C)

12-cup muffin tin, greased or paper-lined

1. In a bowl combine wheat germ, oats, flour, baking powder, salt, cinnamon, nutmeg and brown sugar; blend well. With a pastry blender or 2 knives, cut in shortening; mix until crumbly. Add egg, milk and vanilla; stir just until moist.

2. Spoon batter into prepared muffin tin, filling three-quarters full. Bake in preheated oven for 15 to 20 minutes.

orange-glazed wheat germ muffins

Preheat oven to 400° F (200° C)
12-cup muffin tin, greased or paper-lined

ORANGE GLAZE

1/2 cup	confectioner's sugar (icing sugar)	125 mL
1 tbsp	orange juice	15 mL

1 1/2 cups	all-purpose flour	375 mL
1/2 cup	wheat germ	125 mL
1/4 cup	granulated sugar	50 mL
1 tbsp	baking powder	15 mL
1/2 tsp	salt	2 mL
1 tbsp	grated orange zest	15 mL
2/3 cup	milk	150 mL
1/3 cup	margarine, melted	75 mL
2	eggs	2

1. In a bowl combine sugar and orange juice; blend well. Set aside.

2. In another bowl combine flour, wheat germ, sugar, baking powder, salt and zest; mix well. Make a well in the center.

3. In another bowl combine milk, margarine and eggs. Add to dry ingredients; stir just until moist and blended.

4. Spoon batter into prepared muffin tin, filling to top. Bake in preheated oven for 20 to 25 minutes. Let cool; drizzle with glaze.

spicy whole wheat muffins

Preheat oven to 350° F (180° C)
Muffin tin, greased or paper-lined

2 cups	whole wheat flour	500 mL
3/4 cup	all-purpose flour	175 mL
2/3 cup	packed brown sugar	150 mL
2 tsp	baking soda	10 mL
1 tsp	pumpkin pie spice	5 mL
2 cups	buttermilk	500 mL
3/4 cup	raisins	175 mL

1. In a bowl combine whole wheat flour, all-purpose flour, brown sugar, baking soda and pumpkin pie spice; blend well. Add buttermilk; stir just until moist. Fold in raisins.

2. Spoon batter into prepared muffin tin, dividing evenly. Bake in preheated oven for 35 to 40 minutes.

apricot whole wheat muffins

1	can (14 oz [398 mL]) apricot halves, well-drained	1
1 cup	all-purpose flour	250 mL
3/4 cup	whole wheat flour	175 mL
2 1/2 tsp	baking powder	12 mL
1/2 tsp	baking soda	2 mL
3/4 tsp	salt	4 mL
Pinch	ginger	Pinch
1/3 cup	brown sugar	75 mL
1	egg	1
1/4 cup	oil	50 mL
1/2 cup	milk	125 mL
1/4 cup	dried apricot halves, cut into tiny pieces	50 mL

Preheat oven to 400° F (200° C)
12-cup muffin tin, greased or paper-lined

1. In a blender purée canned apricots. Set aside.

2. In a bowl combine all-purpose flour, whole wheat flour, baking powder, baking soda, salt, ginger and brown sugar; mix well. Make a well in the center.

3. In another bowl whisk together egg, oil and milk. Add 1 cup (250 mL) apricot purée and dried apricots. Add to flour mixture; stir just until moist and blended.

4. Spoon batter into prepared muffin tin, dividing evenly. Bake in preheated oven for about 15 minutes.

orange marmalade wheat muffins

3/4 cup	whole wheat flour	175 mL
3/4 cup	all-purpose flour	175 mL
1/3 cup	granulated sugar	75 mL
2 tsp	baking powder	10 mL
1/2 tsp	baking soda	2 mL
1/4 tsp	salt	1 mL
2 tsp	ginger	10 mL
2	eggs	2
1/3 cup	sour cream	75 mL
1/3 cup	orange juice	75 mL
7 tbsp	butter, melted	105 mL
1 tbsp	grated orange zest	15 mL
	Orange marmalade	

Preheat oven to 400° F (200° C)
16-cup muffin tin, greased

1. In a bowl combine whole wheat flour, all-purpose flour, sugar, baking powder, baking soda, salt and ginger. Make a well in the center.

2. In another bowl whisk together eggs, sour cream, orange juice, butter and orange zest. Pour into dry ingredients; stir quickly just until moist and blended.

3. Spoon batter into prepared muffin tin, filling three-quarters full. Add about 1 tsp (5 mL) orange marmalade to center of each. Bake in preheated oven for about 20 minutes.

walnut crunch wheat muffins

1 cup	whole wheat flour	250 mL
1 cup	all-purpose flour	250 mL
1/2 tsp	salt	2 mL
1 tbsp	baking powder	15 mL
1 tsp	baking soda	5 mL
1/2 cup	brown sugar	125 mL
1 cup	coarsely chopped walnuts	250 mL
1 cup	buttermilk	250 mL
2	eggs, beaten	2
1/3 cup	melted butter	75 mL

Preheat oven to 425° F (220° C)

18-cup muffin tin, greased or paper-lined

1. In a bowl sift together whole wheat flour, all-purpose flour, salt, baking powder, baking soda and brown sugar; mix well. Add walnuts; make a well in the center.

2. In another bowl whisk together buttermilk, eggs and butter. Pour into flour mixture; stir only until moist and blended.

3. Spoon batter into prepared muffin tin, filling three-quarters full. Bake in preheated oven for about 15 minutes.

yogurt-honey muffins

1 1/4 cups	whole wheat flour	300 mL
1 cup	all-purpose flour	250 mL
1/4 cup	brown sugar	50 mL
1 1/2 tsp	baking powder	7 mL
1 tsp	baking soda	5 mL
1 tsp	salt	5 mL
Pinch	cinnamon	Pinch
Pinch	nutmeg	Pinch
1 1/2 cups	plain yogurt	375 mL
1/4 cup	honey	50 mL
1/4 cup	melted butter	50 mL
1	egg	1
1 cup	raisins (optional)	250 mL

Preheat oven to 400° F (200° C)

12-cup muffin tin, greased

1. In a bowl combine whole wheat flour, all-purpose flour, brown sugar, baking powder, baking soda, salt, cinnamon and nutmeg; mix well. Make a well in the center.

2. In another bowl whisk together yogurt, honey, butter and egg. Pour into dry ingredients. Fold in raisins; stir just until moist and blended.

3. Spoon batter into prepared muffin tin. Bake in preheated oven for about 15 minutes.

savory yogurt muffins

1 cup	rolled oats	250 mL
1/3 cup	oat bran	75 mL
1 cup	boiling water	250 mL
1 cup	granulated sugar	250 mL
1/3 cup	oil	75 mL
2	eggs	2
2 cups	low-fat yogurt	500 mL
1 cup	whole wheat flour	250 mL
1 cup	all-purpose flour	250 mL
3 tsp	baking soda	15 mL
2 cups	bran cereal	500 mL

Preheat oven to 375° F (190° C)
Muffin tin, greased or paper-lined

1. In a bowl combine oats, bran and water. Let stand for 5 minutes. Add sugar, oil, eggs and yogurt; blend well. Add whole wheat flour, all-purpose flour, baking soda and bran cereal; stir just until blended. Do not overmix.

2. Spoon batter into prepared muffin tin, filling to top. Bake in preheated oven for about 15 minutes.

muffin stuff
If you only want to use half the batter, keep the remainder covered in your refrigerator for up to 2 weeks.

variations
For every 2 cups (500 mL) batter, you can add:
1 cup (250 mL) fresh or frozen berries (blueberries, raspberries or cranberries) and 1 tbsp (15 mL) grated orange zest.

1 cup (250 mL) chopped fruit (dates, raisins, prunes, apricots), 1/2 cup (125 mL) chopped nuts (walnuts or almonds) and 1 tsp (5 mL) pumpkin pie spice.

delicious vegetable muffins

2 1/3 cups	all-purpose flour	575 mL
4 tbsp	grated Parmesan cheese	60 mL
2 tbsp	granulated sugar	25 mL
1 tbsp	baking powder	15 mL
3/4 tsp	salt	4 mL
3/4 tsp	dried thyme	4 mL
1/8 tsp	nutmeg	0.5 mL
1 cup	milk	250 mL
1/4 cup	vegetable oil	50 mL
1	egg	1
1/2 cup	chopped spinach leaves	125 mL
1/2 cup	grated carrots	125 mL
1	scallion, chopped	1
2 tbsp	sliced pimento	25 mL

Preheat oven to 350° F (180° C)
Muffin tin, greased

1. In a bowl combine flour, 2 tbsp (25 mL) Parmesan cheese, sugar, baking powder, salt, thyme and nutmeg.

2. In another bowl combine milk, oil and egg. Add to flour mixture; stir just until moist. Add spinach, carrots, scallion and pimento.

3. Spoon batter into prepared muffin tin, filling three-quarters full. Sprinkle with remaining Parmesan cheese. Bake in preheated oven for 20 to 25 minutes or until toothpick inserted in center comes out clean and dry.

two-tone muffins

2 cups	all-purpose flour	500 mL
1/2 cup	granulated sugar	125 mL
1 tbsp	baking powder	15 mL
1 tsp	salt	5 mL
3/4 cup	roasted diced almonds	175 mL
3/4 cup	orange juice	175 mL
1/3 cup	almond oil *or* vegetable oil	75 mL
1	egg, beaten	1
1/4 cup	cocoa powder	50 mL
1 tsp	grated orange zest	5 mL

Preheat oven to 400° F (200° C)
12-cup muffin tin, paper-lined

1. In a bowl combine flour, sugar, baking powder and salt. Add almonds, reserving some for garnish.

2. In another bowl combine orange juice, oil and egg. Add to flour mixture; stir just until moist.

3. In another bowl combine half the batter and cocoa powder. Set aside. To remaining batter add orange zest; mix well.

4. Spoon orange zest batter into one side of prepared muffin cups, dividing evenly. Spoon cocoa powder batter into other side of cups, dividing evenly. Sprinkle with reserved almonds. Bake in preheated oven for 20 minutes or until toothpick inserted in center comes out clean and dry.

wild rice muffins

2 cups	water	500 mL
1/3 cup	wild rice	75 mL
2	large eggs	2
1 cup	milk	250 mL
1/2 cup	melted butter, cooled	125 mL
1 1/2 cups	all-purpose flour	375 mL
1/2 cup	natural bran	125 mL
1/3 cup	packed brown sugar	75 mL
1 tbsp	baking powder	15 mL
1/4 tsp	salt	1 mL
1/4 tsp	nutmeg	1 mL
1/2 cup	chopped toasted pecans	125 mL
1/2 cup	sliced dates	125 mL
1/4 cup	slivered apricots	50 mL
2 tsp	grated orange zest	10 mL

Preheat oven to 375° F (190° C)
Muffin tin, paper-lined

1. In a saucepan over high heat, bring water to a boil. Reduce heat to medium; add rice. Cook, covered, for 45 minutes or until tender. Drain well; set aside to cool.

2. In a bowl whisk eggs. Add rice, milk and butter; mix well.

3. In another bowl combine flour, bran, brown sugar, baking powder, salt and nutmeg. Add to rice mixture; blend well. Add pecans, dates, apricots and orange zest; mix just until moist.

4. Spoon batter into prepared muffin tin, dividing evenly. Bake in preheated oven for 20 to 25 minutes or until golden brown.

low-fat muffins

all-bran muffins

1 1/4 cups	all-bran cereal	300 mL
1 cup	buttermilk	250 mL
1	egg	1
1/2 cup	vegetable oil	125 mL
2 tbsp	molasses	25 mL
2 tsp	vanilla	10 mL
1 cup	all-purpose flour	250 mL
1 tsp	baking powder	5 mL
1 tsp	baking soda	5 mL
Pinch	salt	Pinch

Preheat oven to 425° F (220° C)
Muffin tin, paper-lined

1. In a bowl cover cereal with buttermilk. Set aside.

2. In another bowl vigorously beat together egg, oil, molasses and vanilla.

3. In another bowl combine flour, baking powder, baking soda and salt. Add to egg mixture; stir just until blended. Add cereal mixture; blend well.

4. Spoon batter into prepared muffin tin, filling three-quarters full. Bake in preheated oven for 15 to 20 minutes.

muffin stuff

As a substitute for 1 cup (250 mL) buttermilk, you can combine 3 tbsp (45 mL) powdered buttermilk with about 3/4 cup (175 mL) lukewarm water.

apricot orange muffins

1 cup	orange juice	250 mL
1/2 cup	chopped dried apricots	125 mL
1/2 cup	raisins	125 mL
1	egg	1
1	egg white	1
2 tbsp	butter, melted	25 mL
1 1/2 tsp	vanilla	7 mL
2 cups	all-purpose flour	500 mL
3/4 cup	granulated sugar	175 mL
2 tsp	baking powder	10 mL
1 tsp	baking soda	5 mL
Pinch	nutmeg	Pinch

Preheat oven to 350° F (180° C)
12-cup muffin tin, lightly sprayed with vegetable spray or paper-lined

1. In a bowl combine orange juice, apricots, raisins, egg, egg white, butter and vanilla.

2. In another bowl combine flour, sugar, baking powder, baking soda and nutmeg. Add liquid ingredients; stir just until moist and blended.

3. Spoon batter into prepared muffin tin, filling three-quarters full. Bake in preheated oven for 20 to 25 minutes or until golden brown.

easy bran muffins

2 tbsp	canola oil	25 mL
1/4 cup	firmly packed brown sugar	50 mL
1/4 cup	molasses	50 mL
2	egg whites	2
1 cup	skim or 1% milk	250 mL
1 1/2 cups	bran	375 mL
1 cup	all-purpose flour	250 mL
1 1/2 tsp	baking powder	7 mL
1/2 tsp	baking soda	2 mL
3/4 tsp	salt	4 mL
1/2 cup	raisins	125 mL

Preheat oven to 400° F (200° C)

12-cup muffin tin, lightly sprayed with vegetable spray or paper-lined

1. In a bowl beat together oil, brown sugar, molasses and egg whites. Add milk and bran; blend well.

2. In another bowl combine flour, baking powder, baking soda and salt. Add to liquid ingredients; stir just until moist. Add raisins; blend.

3. Spoon batter into prepared muffin tin, dividing evenly. Bake in preheated oven for 18 to 20 minutes.

variations

Ginger Bran Muffins: Add 1 tbsp (15 mL) finely chopped crystalized ginger to batter.

old-fashioned bran muffins

1 1/2 cups	skim milk *or* non-fat dry milk	375 mL
1 cup	whole bran cereal	250 mL
1 1/4 cups	all-purpose flour	300 mL
2 tbsp	granulated sugar	25 mL
4 tsp	double-acting baking powder	20 mL
3/4 tsp	salt	4 mL
1	egg	1
3 tbsp	shortening, melted	45 mL

Preheat oven to 400° F (200° C)

18-cup muffin tin, lightly sprayed with vegetable spray or paper-lined

1. In a bowl cover bran cereal with milk. Let stand for 5 minutes.

2. In another bowl combine flour, sugar, baking powder and salt. Make a well in the center.

3. Add egg and shortening to bran mixture; blend well. Pour into flour mixture; stir just until moist and blended.

4. Spoon batter into prepared muffin tin, dividing evenly. Bake in preheated oven for 25 minutes or until brown.

banana bran muffins

2 1/2 cups	whole wheat flour	625 mL
1/2 cup	coarsely chopped dates	125 mL
1/2 cup	coarsely chopped prunes	125 mL
3 cups	bran	750 mL
1 cup	boiling water	250 mL
1 cup	raisins	250 mL
2 1/2 tsp	baking soda	12 mL
1 cup	buttermilk *or* low-fat milk	250 mL
3/4 cup	honey	175 mL
2	ripe bananas, mashed	2
1/3 cup	oil	75 mL
1/2 cup	egg substitute	125 mL
1/2 cup	chopped walnuts (optional)	125 mL

Preheat oven to 350° F (180° C)
20-cup muffin tin, lightly sprayed with vegetable spray or paper-lined

1. In a food processor combine 1 cup (250 mL) flour, dates and prunes; process until finely chopped. In a bowl combine fruit mixture, bran, water and raisins. Let stand for 10 minutes.

2. In another bowl combine remaining flour and baking soda.

3. In another bowl, combine buttermilk, honey, bananas, oil, egg substitute and walnuts; blend well. Add to flour mixture; combine well. Add bran mixture; stir just until moist and blended.

4. Spoon batter into prepared muffin tin, filling three-quarters full. Bake in preheated oven for 20 to 25 minutes.

raisin bran muffins

1/2 cup	whole wheat flour	125 mL
1/4 cup + 3 tbsp	all-purpose flour	50 mL + 45 mL
6 tsp	sugar substitute	30 mL
1 tbsp	baking powder	15 mL
1/4 tsp	salt	1 mL
1 1/2 cups	unprocessed bran	375 mL
1 1/2 cups	uncooked quick-cooking rolled oats	375 mL
3/4 cup	buttermilk	175 mL
1/4 cup	frozen, concentrated apple juice	50 mL
2 tbsp	vegetable oil	25 mL
2	egg whites	2
2 1/2 tsp	honey	12 mL
1/4 cup + 2 tbsp	raisins	50 mL + 25 mL
1/2 cup	hot water	125 mL

Preheat oven to 400° F (200° C)
12-cup muffin tin, lightly sprayed with vegetable spray or paper-lined

1. In a bowl sift together whole wheat flour, all-purpose flour, sugar substitute, baking powder and salt; blend well. Add bran and oats.

2. In a blender combine buttermilk, apple juice, oil, egg whites and honey; process until well blended. Pour into dry ingredients; stir just until moist. Add raisins and hot water.

3. Spoon batter into prepared muffin tin, filling three-quarters full. Bake in preheated oven for 20 minutes or until lightly browned and firm to the touch.

blueberry muffins

1 3/4 cups	all-purpose flour	425 mL
3 tsp	baking powder	15 mL
1/2 tsp	salt	2 mL
3 tbsp	granulated sugar	45 mL
1	egg white	1
1 tsp	lemon juice	5 mL
1 cup	skim milk	250 mL
1/4 cup	corn oil margarine, melted	50 mL
1 cup	frozen unsweetened blueberries, not thawed	250 mL

Preheat oven to 400° F (200° C)
Muffin tin, lightly sprayed with vegetable spray or paper-lined

1. In a bowl sift together flour, baking powder, salt and sugar.

2. In another bowl beat together egg white and lemon juice until stiff.

3. Add milk and margarine to flour mixture; blend with a fork just until mixed. Fold in beaten egg white. Add blueberries.

4. Spoon batter into prepared muffin tin, filling three-quarters full. Bake in preheated oven for 25 minutes.

blueberry buttermilk bran muffins

3 cups	bran	750 mL
2 cups	whole wheat flour	500 mL
3/4 cup	granulated sugar	175 mL
1 tbsp	baking powder	15 mL
1 tsp	baking soda	5 mL
2	eggs, beaten	2
2 cups	buttermilk	500 mL
1/2 cup	vegetable oil	125 mL
1/2 cup	molasses	125 mL
1 cup	fresh or frozen blueberries	250 mL

Preheat oven to 375° F (190° C)
Muffin tin, paper-lined

1. In a bowl combine bran, flour, sugar, baking powder and baking soda.

2. In another bowl combine eggs, buttermilk, oil and molasses. Pour into dry ingredients; stir just until moist. Do not overmix. Fold in blueberries.

3. Spoon batter into prepared muffin tin, filling three-quarters full. Bake in preheated oven for about 25 minutes.

blueberry oatmeal muffins

1 3/4 cups	all-purpose flour	425 mL
1 cup	quick-cooking rolled oats	250 mL
1/4 cup	firmly packed brown sugar	50 mL
1 tbsp	baking powder	15 mL
1/2 tsp	salt	2 mL
1 tsp	cinnamon	5 mL
1 cup	skim milk	250 mL
1	egg, beaten	1
3 tbsp	oil	45 mL
1 cup	fresh or frozen blueberries, unsweetened	250 mL

Preheat oven to 425° F (220° C)
12-cup muffin tin, paper-lined

1. In a bowl combine flour, oats, brown sugar, baking powder, salt and cinnamon; blend well. Add milk, egg and oil; stir until blended. Fold in berries.

2. Spoon batter into prepared muffin tin, dividing evenly. Bake in preheated oven for 20 to 25 minutes.

herbed brown rice muffins

1 3/4 cups + 2 tbsp	all-purpose flour	425 mL + 25 mL
1 cup	cooked brown rice	250 mL
1 tbsp	baking powder	15 mL
2 tsp	granulated sugar	10 mL
1/2 tsp	salt	2 mL
1/4 cup	minced fresh basil	50 mL
2 tbsp	chopped fresh dill	25 mL
1 cup	skim milk	250 mL
1/4 cup	water	50 mL
1	egg	1
3 tbsp	vegetable oil	45 mL

Preheat oven to 400° F (200° C)
12-cup muffin tin, paper-lined

1. In a bowl combine flour, rice, baking powder, sugar, salt, basil and dill; blend well with a fork.

2. In another bowl combine milk, water, egg and oil. Add to flour mixture; stir just until blended.

3. Spoon batter into prepared muffin tin, dividing evenly. Bake in preheated oven for 20 to 25 minutes.

carrot orange muffins

1 cup	all-purpose flour	250 mL
1 cup	whole wheat flour	250 mL
2 tsp	baking powder	10 mL
1 tsp	cinnamon	5 mL
1/4 tsp	salt	1 mL
1 tsp	grated orange zest	5 mL
1/2 cup + 2 tbsp	fresh orange juice	125 mL + 25 mL
1/2 cup	skim milk	125 mL
1/4 cup	vegetable oil	50 mL
2 tbsp	honey	25 mL
2	egg whites	2
1 cup	coarsely grated carrots	250 mL

Preheat oven to 400° F (200° C)
Muffin tin, lightly sprayed with vegetable spray or paper-lined

1. In a bowl combine all-purpose flour, whole wheat flour, baking powder, cinnamon and salt.

2. In another bowl whisk together orange zest, orange juice, milk, oil, honey and egg whites (mixture will look curdled.) Add carrots; pour into flour mixture. Fold with spatula just until moist.

3. Spoon batter into prepared muffin tin, filling three-quarters full. Bake in preheated oven for 20 to 25 minutes or until golden brown.

carrot raisin muffins

1/2 cup	all-purpose flour	125 mL
1/2 cup	whole wheat flour	125 mL
1 tsp	baking powder	5 mL
1/2 tsp	baking soda	2 mL
1 tsp	cinnamon	5 mL
1/4 tsp	salt	1 mL
4	egg whites	4
2/3 cup	granulated sugar	160 mL
1/4 cup	vegetable oil	50 mL
1/2 tsp	vanilla	2 mL
1 1/2 cups	shredded carrots	375 mL
1/2 cup	raisins	125 mL

Preheat oven to 375° F (190° C)
12-cup muffin tin, paper-lined

1. In a bowl combine all-purpose flour, whole wheat flour, baking powder, baking soda, cinnamon and salt.

2. In another bowl whisk together egg whites, sugar, oil and vanilla. Add dry ingredients; stir just until moist. Add carrots and raisins.

3. Spoon batter into prepared muffin tin, filling three-quarters full. Bake in preheated oven for about 20 minutes.

cinnamon raisin muffins

2 1/4 cups	all-purpose flour	550 mL
1/4 cup	granulated sugar	50 mL
2 tsp	baking powder	10 mL
1 tsp	cinnamon	5 mL
1/2 tsp	baking soda	2 mL
1/2 tsp	salt	2 mL
3/4 cup	dark raisins	175 mL
1 cup + 2 tbsp	buttermilk	250 mL + 25 mL
1	egg, lightly beaten	1

Preheat oven to 375° F (190° C)
12-cup muffin tin, paper-lined

1. In a bowl combine flour, sugar, baking powder, cinnamon, baking soda and salt; blend well. Add raisins, buttermilk and egg, mixing just until blended.

2. Spoon batter into prepared muffin tin, filling three-quarters full. Bake in preheated oven for about 20 minutes or until lightly browned.

quick cornmeal muffins

1 cup	cornmeal	250 mL
1/2 cup	whole wheat flour	125 mL
1/2 cup	unbleached flour	125 mL
1 tbsp	baking powder	15 mL
1 tsp	dried sage	5 mL
1 cup	skim milk	250 mL
1/4 cup	fat-free egg substitute	50 mL
2 tbsp	honey	25 mL
2 tbsp	oil	25 mL

Preheat oven to 450° F (230° C)
12-cup muffin tin, sprayed with vegetable spray

1. In a bowl combine cornmeal, whole wheat flour, unbleached flour, baking powder and sage; blend well. Make a well in the center.

2. In another bowl whisk together milk, egg substitute, honey and oil. Pour into dry ingredients; stir until well blended.

3. Spoon batter into prepared muffin tin, filling two-thirds full. Bake in preheated oven for 15 minutes or until golden brown.

low-cal cornmeal muffins

3/4 cup	cornmeal	175 mL
1/4 cup	all-purpose flour	50 mL
1/2 tsp	salt	2 mL
1 1/2 tsp	baking powder	7 mL
1/4 tsp	baking soda	1 mL
3/4 cup	buttermilk	175 mL
1	egg	1
2 tbsp	butter or margarine, melted or vegetable oil	25 mL
2 tbsp	sugar substitute	25 mL

Preheat oven to 425° F (220° C)
Muffin tin, paper-lined

1. In a bowl sift together cornmeal, flour, salt, baking powder and baking soda; blend well. Add buttermilk, egg, butter and sugar substitute; beat for 1 minute with rotary beater (mixture will be loose.)

2. Spoon batter into prepared muffin tin, filling three-quarters full. Bake in preheated oven for 20 to 25 minutes.

johnny appleseed muffins

1 cup	whole wheat flour	250 mL
1/2 cup	unbleached flour	125 mL
1 cup	bran flakes cereal	250 mL
1 tbsp	baking powder	15 mL
1/2 tsp	baking soda	2 mL
1 tsp	cinnamon	5 mL
1/2 tsp	grated nutmeg	2 mL
1/2 tsp	ground cloves	2 mL
1 1/4 cups	applesauce	300 mL
1/2 cup	fat-free egg substitute	125 mL
1/3 cup	honey	75 mL
2 tbsp	oil	25 mL
1	medium apple, shredded	1

Preheat oven to 425° F (220° C)

12-cup muffin tin, sprayed with vegetable spray or paper-lined

1. In a bowl combine whole wheat flour, unbleached flour, cereal, baking powder, baking soda, cinnamon, nutmeg and cloves; mix well.

2. In another bowl whisk together applesauce, egg substitute, honey and oil; blend well. Add apple; pour into flour mixture. Stir just until moist.

3. Spoon batter into prepared muffin tin. Bake in preheated oven for about 20 minutes.

maple muffins

1 cup	whole wheat flour	250 mL
1 cup	unbleached flour	250 mL
1/4 cup	coarsely chopped pecans	50 mL
2 tsp	baking powder	10 mL
2/3 cup	low-fat milk	160 mL
2/3 cup	maple syrup	160 mL
1/2 cup	fat-free egg substitute	125 mL
2 tbsp	oil	25 mL

Preheat oven to 375° F (190° C)

12-cup muffin tin, sprayed with vegetable spray

1. In a bowl combine whole wheat flour, unbleached flour, pecans and baking powder.

2. In another bowl whisk together milk, maple syrup, egg substitute and oil. Pour into dry ingredients; stir just until blended.

3. Spoon batter into prepared muffin tin, filling three-quarters full. Bake in preheated oven for 15 to 20 minutes.

maple pecan muffins

1 cup	all purpose flour	250 mL
1/2 cup	whole wheat flour	125 mL
1/4 cup	chopped pecans	50 mL
2	egg yolks	2
1/2 cup	skim milk	125 mL
1/4 cup	maple syrup	50 mL
2 tbsp	unsalted butter or margarine, melted	25 mL
4	egg whites	4
3 tbsp	granulated sugar	45 mL

Preheat oven to 400° F (200° C)
Muffin tin, paper-lined

1. In a bowl combine all-purpose flour, whole wheat flour and pecans. Set aside.

2. In another bowl combine egg yolks, milk, maple syrup and melted butter. Set aside.

3. In another bowl beat egg whites at high speed, gradually adding sugar, until stiff peaks form.

4. Beat milk mixture until well blended. Add to flour mixture; stir until moist. Gently fold in egg whites until blended.

5. Spoon batter into prepared muffin tin, filling to top. Bake in preheated oven for 20 minutes or until lightly browned.

orange currant oat bran muffins

2 1/2 cups	oat bran	625 mL
1/2 cup	currants	125 mL
1 tbsp	baking powder	15 mL
1 tsp	grated orange zest	5 mL
1/3 cup	granulated sugar	75 mL
1/2 cup	fresh orange juice	125 mL
1/4 cup	vegetable oil	50 mL
3	egg whites	3

Preheat oven to 375° F (190° C)
Muffin tin, sprayed with vegetable spray

1. In a bowl combine oat bran, currants, baking powder, orange zest and 1/4 cup (50 mL) sugar; blend well. Add orange juice and oil; stir until well blended.

2. In a bowl beat egg whites; slowly add remaining sugar until soft peaks form. Gently add to oat bran mixture; blend well.

3. Spoon batter into prepared muffin tin, dividing evenly. Bake in preheated oven for about 20 minutes or until browned.

orange fig fiber muffins

1	small orange, cut into quarters and seeds removed	1
3/4 cup	water	175 mL
5	large dried figs, cut into quarters	5
1/4 cup	margarine, cut into pieces	50 mL
1/4 cup + 2 tbsp	frozen orange juice concentrate	50 mL + 25 mL
2	egg whites	2
2 cups less 2 tbsp	all-purpose flour	500 mL less 25 mL
1 tsp	baking powder	5 mL
1/2 tsp	baking soda	2 mL
1/2 tsp	salt	2 mL
2 1/2 tsp	sunflower seeds	12 mL

Preheat oven to 350° F (180° C)
Muffin tin, paper-lined

1. In a blender or food processor combine orange, water, figs, margarine, orange juice concentrate and egg whites. Process for 1 minute or until well blended and peel is finely ground. Transfer to a bowl.

2. In another bowl sift together flour, baking powder, baking soda and salt. Add to orange mixture; stir just until blended. Fold in sunflower seeds.

3. Spoon batter into prepared muffin tin, dividing evenly. Bake in preheated oven for about 35 minutes.

sunny boy cereal muffins

1 cup	sifted whole wheat flour	250 mL
1 cup	Sunny Boy cereal	250 mL
1/2 cup	raisins or chopped dates	125 mL
1/2 tsp	salt	2 mL
1/2 cup	honey	125 mL
2 tbsp	safflower oil	25 mL
1	egg	1
1 tsp	baking soda	5 mL
1 cup	buttermilk or sour milk	250 mL

Preheat oven to 375° F (190° C)
Muffin tin, paper-lined

1. In a bowl combine flour, cereal, raisins and salt; blend well.

2. In another bowl combine honey, oil and egg; mix well.

3. In another bowl combine baking soda and buttermilk; blend well. Add to honey mixture; mix well. Add to flour mixture; stir just until moist.

4. Spoon batter into prepared muffin tin, dividing evenly. Bake in preheated oven for about 25 minutes.

pineapple bran muffins

4	egg whites	4
1	can (8 oz [227 mL]) crushed pineapple, in juice	1
1/2 cup	granulated sugar	125 mL
1/3 cup	skim or 1% milk	75 mL
3 tbsp	vegetable oil	45 mL
3 tbsp	molasses	45 mL
1 1/2 cups	wheat bran or all-bran cereal or whole bran flakes	375 mL
3/4 cup	all-purpose flour	175 mL
3/4 cup	whole wheat flour	175 mL
2 tsp	baking powder	10 mL
1/2 tsp	ginger	2 mL
1/2 tsp	salt	2 mL

Preheat oven to 375° F (190° C)
12-cup muffin tin, sprayed with vegetable spray

1. In a bowl whisk together egg whites, pineapple (with juice), sugar, milk, oil and molasses; blend well. Add bran. Let stand for 5 minutes.

2. In another bowl combine all-purpose flour, whole wheat flour, baking powder, ginger and salt. Add to bran mixture; stir just until blended.

3. Spoon batter into prepared muffin tin. Bake in preheated oven for 20 to 25 minutes.

prune muffins

1 cup	prune paste	250 mL
2 cups	brown sugar	500 mL
2	eggs	2
2 tbsp	molasses	25 mL
2 3/4 cups	all-purpose flour	675 mL
1 1/2 cups	wheat bran	375 mL
2 tsp	baking powder	10 mL
1/2 tsp	salt	2 mL
1 cup	raisins	250 mL
2 tsp	baking soda	10 mL
2 cups	buttermilk	500 mL

Preheat oven to 375° F (190° C)
18-cup muffin tin, sprayed with vegetable spray or paper-lined

1. In a bowl beat together prune paste and sugar. Add eggs and molasses; beat well.

2. In another bowl combine flour, bran, baking powder and salt. Add to prune mixture; stir just until blended. Add raisins.

3. In another bowl combine baking soda and buttermilk; mix well. Add to batter; stir just until blended.

4. Spoon batter into prepared muffin tin, filling two-thirds full. Bake in preheated oven for about 20 minutes.

fruit muffins

apple muffins

2 1/4 cups	sifted cake flour	550 mL
3 1/2 tsp	baking powder	17 mL
1/2 tsp	salt	2 mL
1/2 tsp	cinnamon	2 mL
1/2 tsp	nutmeg	2 mL
4 tbsp	shortening	60 mL
1/2 cup	granulated sugar	125 mL
1	egg, beaten	1
1 cup	milk	250 mL
1 cup	finely chopped peeled apples	250 mL
2 tbsp	granulated sugar	25 mL

Preheat oven to 425° F (220° C)
Muffin tin, greased or paper-lined

1. In a bowl sift together flour, baking powder, salt, 1/4 tsp (1 mL) cinnamon and 1/4 tsp (1 mL) nutmeg; blend well.

2. In another bowl cream together shortening and sugar. Add egg; stir well. Add flour mixture alternately with milk; combine well. Fold in apples.

3. Spoon batter into prepared muffin tin, filling three-quarters full. Sprinkle tops with sugar and remaining cinnamon and nutmeg. Bake in preheated oven for 20 to 25 minutes.

cheesy apple bacon muffins

2 cups	all-purpose flour	500 mL
1/4 cup	granulated sugar	50 mL
4 tsp	baking powder	20 mL
3/4 tsp	salt	4 mL
1 cup	milk	250 mL
1/3 cup	melted butter	75 mL
1	egg, slightly beaten	1
1/2 cup	finely chopped unpeeled apples	250 mL
3/4 cup	grated old Cheddar cheese	175 mL
2/3 cup	crumbled crisp bacon (about 8 slices)	150 mL

Preheat oven to 400° F (200° C)
18-cup muffin tin, greased or paper-lined

1. In a bowl combine flour, sugar, baking powder and salt; blend well.

2. In another bowl combine milk, butter and egg; mix well. Add to flour mixture; stir just until blended. Fold in apples, cheese and bacon.

3. Spoon batter into prepared muffin tin, dividing evenly. Bake in preheated oven for 15 to 20 minutes or until browned.

spicy apple bran muffins

4	eggs	4
1 1/2 cups	milk	375 mL
1 cup	packed brown sugar	250 mL
1/2 cup	vegetable oil	125 mL
2 tsp	vanilla	10 mL
3 cups	bran cereal	750 mL
2 cups	grated peeled apples	500 mL
1 cup	raisins	250 mL
1 cup	chopped walnuts	250 mL
3 cups	all-purpose flour	750 mL
2 tbsp	baking powder	25 mL
2 tsp	baking soda	10 mL
1 1/2 tsp	cinnamon	7 mL
1/2 tsp	nutmeg	2 mL
1 tsp	salt	5 mL

Preheat oven to 375° F (190° C)
Muffin tin, greased or paper-lined

1. In a bowl beat eggs. Add milk, brown sugar, oil and vanilla; blend well. Add bran cereal, apples, raisins and walnuts; mix well.

2. In another bowl combine flour, baking powder, baking soda, cinnamon, nutmeg and salt. Add bran mixture; mix well. Add to flour mixture; stir just until blended.

3. Spoon batter into prepared muffin tin, dividing evenly. Bake in preheated oven for 20 minutes or until firm to the touch.

applecrisp muffins

1	egg	1
1 1/4 cups	milk	300 mL
1/2 cup	melted margarine	125 mL
1/3 cup	liquid honey	75 mL
1 1/2 cups	graham cracker crumbs	375 mL
1 1/2 cups	all-purpose flour	375 mL
1 tbsp	baking powder	15 mL
1 tsp	cinnamon	5 mL
1/2 tsp	salt	2 mL
1 cup	grated peeled apples	250 mL

Preheat oven to 400° F (200° C)
12-cup muffin tin, greased or paper-lined

1. In a bowl beat egg with a fork. Add milk, margarine and honey; blend well. Add graham crumbs.

2. In another bowl combine flour, baking powder, cinnamon and salt. Add honey mixture; stir just until moist. Fold in apples.

3. Spoon batter into prepared muffin tin, filling to top. Bake in preheated oven for 20 minutes.

apple cinnamon muffins

2 cups	all-purpose flour	500 mL
1/2 cup	granulated sugar	125 mL
3 tsp	baking powder	15 mL
1/2 tsp	cinnamon	2 mL
1/2 tsp	salt	2 mL
1/2 cup	butter *or* margarine	125 mL
1	large apple, peeled and diced	1
1/4 cup	finely chopped walnuts	50 mL
1	egg	1
2/3 cup	milk	150 mL
1 tsp	cinnamon	5 mL
1 tbsp	brown sugar	15 mL

Preheat oven to 425° F (220° C)
16-cup muffin tin, greased

1. In a bowl sift together flour, sugar, baking powder, cinnamon and salt. With a pastry blender or 2 knives cut in butter. Measure out 1/4 cup (50 mL) mixture; reserve for topping. Add apple and walnuts to remaining flour mixture.

2. In a bowl beat egg. Add milk; blend well. Add to flour mixture; stir just until blended (batter should be lumpy.)

3. Spoon batter into prepared muffin tin, filling two-thirds full. Add cinnamon and brown sugar to reserved topping mixture; sprinkle over batter. Bake in preheated oven for 15 to 20 minutes or until toothpick inserted in center comes out clean.

apple pecan streusel muffins

STREUSEL TOPPING

1/2 cup	brown sugar	125 mL
1/4 cup	butter	50 mL
1/2 cup	chopped pecans	125 mL
2 cups	all-purpose flour	500 mL
2 tsp	baking powder	10 mL
2 tsp	baking soda	10 mL
1 tsp	salt	5 mL
1 tsp	cinnamon	5 mL
1/2 tsp	allspice	2 mL
Pinch	cloves	Pinch
1	egg	1
1 cup	brown sugar	250 mL
1/4 cup	oil	50 mL
1 cup	applesauce	250 mL

Preheat oven to 375° F (190° C)
12-cup muffin tin, greased

1. In a bowl combine brown sugar, butter and pecans; mix until crumbly. Set aside.

2. In another bowl combine flour, baking powder, baking soda, salt, cinnamon, allspice and cloves.

3. In another bowl beat together egg, brown sugar, oil and applesauce. Add to flour mixture; stir just until moist.

4. Spoon batter into prepared muffin tin, filling three-quarters full. Sprinkle with topping. Bake in preheated oven for 20 to 25 minutes or until browned.

spiced apple muffins

2 cups	all-purpose flour	500 mL
1 cup	bran flakes	250 mL
2/3 cup	packed brown sugar	150 mL
3 tsp	baking powder	15 mL
1 tsp	salt	5 mL
1/2 tsp	cinnamon	2 mL
1/4 tsp	nutmeg	1 mL
2	eggs	2
2/3 cup	milk	150 mL
1/4 cup	oil	50 mL
1 cup	grated peeled apples	250 mL

Preheat oven to 400° F (200° C)
16-cup muffin tin, greased

1. In a bowl combine flour, bran flakes, brown sugar, baking powder, salt, cinnamon and nutmeg; blend with a fork. Make a well in the center.

2. In another bowl beat eggs slightly. Add milk, oil and apples; mix well. Add to dry ingredients; stir quickly just until moist (batter will be lumpy.)

3. Spoon batter into prepared muffin tin, filling three-quarters full. Bake in preheated oven for 15 to 20 minutes.

oatmeal raisin apple-sauce muffins

1/2 cup	butter or margarine	125 mL
3/4 cup	lightly packed light brown sugar	175 mL
1	egg	1
1 cup	all-purpose flour	250 mL
1/2 tsp	ground cardamom or cinnamon	2 mL
1 tsp	baking powder	5 mL
1/4 tsp	baking soda	1 mL
1/4 tsp	salt	1 mL
3/4 cup	applesauce	175 mL
1/2 cup	golden raisins	125 mL
1 cup	quick-cooking rolled oats (not instant)	250 mL
1/2 cup	chopped nuts	125 mL
	Icing sugar (optional)	

Preheat oven to 350° F (180° C)
12-cup muffin tin, greased or paper-lined

1. In a bowl cream together butter and brown sugar until light and fluffy. Add egg; beat well.

2. In another bowl combine flour, cardamom, baking powder, baking soda and salt. Add to creamed mixture alternately with applesauce; blend well. Add raisins, oats and nuts.

3. Spoon batter into prepared muffin tin, filling three-quarters full. Bake in preheated oven for 25 to 30 minutes. Let cool. Remove muffins from pan. If desired, sprinkle with icing sugar.

apple streusel muffins

STREUSEL TOPPING

1/3 cup	packed brown sugar	75 mL
2 tbsp	all-purpose flour	25 mL
1/2 tsp	cinnamon	2 mL
2 tbsp	softened butter	25 mL
1/3 cup	chopped pecans (optional)	75 mL

1 1/2 cups	all-purpose flour	375 mL
1/4 cup	granulated sugar	50 mL
2 tsp	baking powder	10 mL
1/2 tsp	cinnamon	2 mL
1/4 tsp	salt	1 mL
1/8 tsp	nutmeg	0.5 mL
1 cup	shredded peeled apples	250 mL
1/2 cup	milk	125 mL
1/4 cup	vegetable oil	50 mL
1	egg, beaten	1

Preheat oven to 400° F (200° C)
12-cup muffin tin, greased or paper-lined

1. In a bowl combine brown sugar, flour, cinnamon, butter and pecans; mix until crumbly. Set aside.

2. In another bowl sift together flour, sugar, baking powder, cinnamon, salt and nutmeg; blend well. Add apples. Make a well in the center.

3. In another bowl combine milk, oil and egg. Add to dry ingredients; stir just until moist.

4. Spoon batter into prepared muffin tin, filling half full. Sprinkle with topping, reserving 3 tbsp (45 mL). Top with remaining batter; sprinkle with remaining topping. Bake in preheated oven for 20 to 25 minutes.

pumpernickel apple-sauce muffins

1 cup	unsweetened applesauce	250 mL
1/4 cup	vegetable oil	50 mL
1	large egg	1
2 tbsp	packed brown sugar	25 mL
2	slices packaged soft pumpernickel bread, torn into small pieces	2
2/3 cup	fine graham cracker crumbs, crushed	150 mL
1/3 cup	all-purpose flour	75 mL
1 tsp	baking soda	5 mL

Preheat oven to 400° F (200° C)
Muffin tin, greased or paper-lined

1. In a food processor combine applesauce, oil, egg and brown sugar; process until well blended. Add bread; continue to process until smooth, stopping once to scrape down sides of container. Add crumbs, flour and baking soda; process until smooth.

2. Spoon batter into prepared muffin tin, filling two-thirds full. Bake in preheated oven for 15 to 20 minutes or until toothpick inserted in center comes out clean.

lemony apricot jam muffins

Preheat oven to 400° F (200° C)
Muffin tin, greased or paper-lined

1 1/2 cups	all-purpose flour	375 mL
1/2 cup	granulated sugar	125 mL
1/2 tsp	grated lemon zest	2 mL
1 1/2 tsp	baking powder	7 mL
1/2 tsp	baking soda	2 mL
1/2 tsp	salt	2 mL
1	egg, beaten	1
4 tbsp	butter, melted	50 mL
1 cup	buttermilk	250 mL
2 tsp	lemon juice	10 mL
TOPPING		
	Apricot jam	
1/4 cup	chopped almonds	50 mL

1. In a bowl combine flour, sugar, lemon zest, baking powder, baking soda and salt. Make a well in the center.

2. In another bowl whisk together egg, butter, buttermilk and lemon juice. Add to dry ingredients; stir just until blended.

3. Spoon batter into prepared muffin tin, filling half full. Drop a bit of apricot jam into each tin. Top with remaining batter; sprinkle with almonds. Bake in preheated oven for 15 to 20 minutes or until golden brown.

iced banana muffins

Preheat oven to 350° F (180° C)
Muffin tin, greased or paper-lined

1 cup	granulated sugar	250 mL
1 tsp	baking soda	5 mL
2 tsp	baking powder	10 mL
2 cups	all-purpose flour	500 mL
Pinch	salt	Pinch
1/2 cup	melted butter	125 mL
2	eggs	2
4 tbsp	milk	60 mL
3	bananas, mashed	3
ICING		
1 1/2 cups	icing sugar	375 mL
2 tbsp	butter, melted	25 mL
1 tsp	vanilla	5 mL
1 1/4 tbsp	milk	19 mL

1. In a bowl sift together sugar, baking soda, baking powder, flour and salt; blend well. Add butter, eggs and milk; stir just until blended. Add bananas.

2. Spoon batter into prepared muffin tin, filling three-quarters full. Bake in preheated oven for 25 minutes. Set aside to cool.

3. In a bowl combine icing sugar, butter, vanilla and milk; mix well. Spread over muffins.

easy banana bran muffins

1 cup	all-purpose flour	250 mL
3 tbsp	granulated sugar	45 mL
2 1/2 tsp	baking powder	12 mL
1/2 tsp	salt	2 mL
1 cup	all-bran cereal	250 mL
1	egg, beaten	1
1 cup	mashed ripe banana	250 mL
1/4 cup	milk	50 mL
2 tbsp	salad oil	25 mL

Preheat oven to 400° F (200° C)
12-cup muffin tin, greased or paper-lined

1. In a bowl sift together flour, sugar, baking powder and salt. Add bran.

2. In another bowl combine egg, banana, milk and oil; blend well. Add to dry ingredients; stir just until moist.

3. Spoon batter into prepared muffin tin, filling three-quarters full. Bake in preheated oven for 20 to 25 minutes.

breakfast special banana chip muffins

1/4 cup	granulated sugar	50 mL
1/4 cup	vegetable oil	50 mL
1 cup	mashed bananas	250 mL
1	egg	1
1 tsp	vanilla	5 mL
1/2 cup	all-bran cereal	125 mL
1/2 cup	all-purpose flour	125 mL
1/2 cup	whole wheat flour	125 mL
1 tsp	baking powder	5 mL
1 tsp	baking soda	5 mL
1/2 tsp	salt	2 mL
1/2 cup	chocolate chips	125 mL

Preheat oven to 375° F (190° C)
Muffin tin, greased or paper-lined

1. In a bowl combine sugar, oil, bananas, egg, vanilla and cereal. Let stand for 5 minutes.

2. In another bowl combine all-purpose flour, whole wheat flour, baking powder, baking soda and salt. Add to bran mixture; stir just until blended. Fold in chocolate chips.

3. Spoon batter into prepared muffin tin, filling three-quarters full. Bake in preheated oven for 20 to 25 minutes.

chocolate 'n' banana muffins

1/3 cup	vegetable oil	75 mL
1/2 cup	granulated sugar	125 mL
1	egg	1
1 cup	mashed bananas	250 mL
1	pkg (10 oz [300 g]) semi-sweet chocolate chips	1
1 cup	all-purpose flour	250 mL
1 tsp	baking soda	5 mL
1/2 tsp	salt	2 mL
1/2 tsp	cinnamon	2 mL

Preheat oven to 350° F (180° C)
12-cup muffin tin, greased or paper-lined

1. In a bowl whisk together oil, sugar and egg. Add bananas and half chocolate chips; mix well.

2. In another bowl combine flour, baking soda, salt and cinnamon. Add to liquid ingredients; stir just until blended.

3. Spoon batter into prepared muffin tin, filling three-quarters full. Sprinkle evenly with remaining chips. Bake in preheated oven for 15 to 20 minutes.

banana nut muffins

1 3/4 cups	all-purpose flour	425 mL
1/3 cup	granulated sugar	75 mL
3 tsp	baking powder	15 mL
1/2 tsp	salt	2 mL
1/2 tsp	nutmeg	2 mL
1/2 cup	chopped nuts	125 mL
1 cup	mashed ripe bananas	250 mL
1/3 cup	salad oil	75 mL
1/4 cup	milk	50 mL
1	egg	1
2 tsp	lemon juice	10 mL

Preheat oven to 400° F (200° C)
12-cup muffin tin, greased

1. In a bowl combine flour, sugar, baking powder, salt and nutmeg; blend well. Add nuts; stir.

2. In another bowl combine bananas, oil, milk, egg and lemon juice. Beat slightly with a rotary beater. Add to dry ingredients; mix just until moist.

3. Spoon batter into prepared muffin tin. Bake in preheated oven for 20 to 25 minutes.

banana 'n' peanut muffins

1 1/2 cups	whole wheat flour	375 mL
2 tsp	baking powder	10 mL
1/2 tsp	baking soda	2 mL
1/2 tsp	salt	2 mL
Pinch	cinnamon	Pinch
Pinch	nutmeg	Pinch
1/2 cup	brown sugar	125 mL
1 1/2 cups	mashed bananas	375 mL
1	egg	1
1/3 cup	melted butter, cooled	75 mL
1/2 cup	coarsely chopped peanuts	125 mL

Preheat oven to 400° F (200° C)
Muffin tin, greased or paper-lined

1. In a bowl combine flour, baking powder, baking soda, salt, cinnamon, nutmeg and brown sugar; stir with a fork until well blended. Make a well in the center.

2. In another bowl whisk together bananas, egg and butter. Add to dry ingredients; fold in nuts. Stir just until moist (batter will be lumpy.)

3. Spoon batter into prepared muffin tin, filling three-quarters full. Bake in preheated oven for about 15 minutes or until toothpick inserted in center comes out clean.

chunky peanut-banana muffins

1	egg	1
1 1/2 cups	milk	375 mL
1/2 cup	crunchy peanut butter	125 mL
1/2 cup	firmly packed brown sugar	125 mL
1/4 cup	vegetable oil	50 mL
1 cup	all-bran cereal	250 mL
2	medium whole bananas, cut into chunks	2
2 cups	all-purpose flour	500 mL
1 tbsp	baking powder	15 mL
1/4 tsp	salt	1 mL

Preheat oven to 400° F (200° C)
Muffin tin, greased or paper-lined

1. In a bowl combine egg, milk, peanut butter, brown sugar and oil; beat until well-blended. Add cereal. Let stand for 5 to 10 minutes. Add bananas.

2. In another bowl combine flour, baking powder and salt. Add cereal mixture; stir just until moist and blended. Batter will be lumpy; do not overmix.

3. Spoon batter into prepared muffin tin, filling to top. Bake in preheated oven for 20 minutes or until golden brown.

banana pineapple muffins

1/2 cup	granulated sugar	125 mL
1/2 cup	softened shortening	125 mL
1/2 cup	mashed overripe bananas	125 mL
1/2 cup	crushed pineapple, with juice	125 mL
1	egg, beaten	1
1 tsp	baking soda	5 mL
1 tsp	baking powder	5 mL
1 1/2 cups	all-purpose flour	375 mL
Pinch	salt	Pinch

Preheat oven to 400° F (200° C)
12-cup muffin tin, greased

1. In a bowl cream together sugar and shortening. Add bananas and pineapple; mix well. Add egg (batter will look curdled.) Add baking soda, baking powder, flour and salt; blend well.

2. Spoon batter into prepared muffin tin, dividing evenly. Bake in preheated oven for 15 minutes.

pineapple-choco-banana muffins

1 cup	all-purpose flour	250 mL
3/4 cup	whole wheat flour	175 mL
1/2 cup	granulated sugar	125 mL
1 cup	semi-sweet chocolate chips	250 mL
1 tbsp	baking powder	15 mL
1/2 tsp	salt	2 mL
1	egg	1
1/2 cup	mashed ripe bananas	125 mL
1	can (14 oz [398 mL]) crushed pineapple, drained, reserve juice	1
1/2 cup	vegetable oil	125 mL

Preheat oven to 375° F (190° C)
Muffin tin, greased or paper-lined

1. In a bowl combine all-purpose flour, whole wheat flour, sugar, chocolate chips, baking powder and salt.

2. In another bowl beat egg. Add bananas, pineapple, reserved juice and oil; stir just until blended. Add to dry ingredients; stir until moist.

3. Spoon batter into prepared muffin tin, filling to top. Bake in preheated oven for 20 to 25 minutes.

very ripe banana muffins

1 cup	mashed overripe bananas	250 mL
1/4 cup + 2 tbsp	vegetable oil	50 mL + 25 mL
1/2 cup	granulated sugar *or* brown sugar	125 mL
1/2 tsp	salt	2 mL
1	egg	1
1 tsp	vanilla	5 mL
1 1/2 cups	all-purpose flour	375 mL
1 tsp	baking soda	5 mL
1 tsp	baking powder	5 mL
1/2 cup	chopped walnuts or pecans (optional)	125 mL

Preheat oven to 350° F (180° C)
Muffin tin, greased or paper-lined

1. In a bowl combine bananas, oil, sugar and salt; blend well. Add egg and vanilla; beat well.

2. In another bowl combine flour, baking soda, baking powder and walnuts. Add to banana mixture; stir just until moist. Do not overmix.

3. Spoon batter into prepared muffin tin, dividing evenly. Bake in preheated oven for 15 to 20 minutes.

banana yogurt muffins

1 2/3 cups	all-purpose flour	410 mL
1 tsp	baking powder	5 mL
1 tsp	baking soda	5 mL
1/2 cup	softened butter	125 mL
2/3 cup	natural bran	150 mL
1/2 cup	chopped nuts	125 mL
1	egg	1
2/3 cup	puréed bananas	160 mL
1/2 cup	plain yogurt	125 mL
1/2 cup	packed brown sugar	125 mL
1 tbsp	molasses	15 mL

Preheat oven to 375° F (190° C)
12-cup muffin tin, greased

1. In a bowl combine flour, baking powder and baking soda. With a pastry blender cut in butter until mixture is crumbly. Add bran and nuts.

2. In another bowl combine egg, bananas, yogurt, sugar and molasses. Add to dry ingredients; stir just until blended.

3. Spoon batter into prepared muffin tin, dividing evenly. Bake in preheated oven for 20 to 25 minutes or until a toothpick inserted in center comes out clean.

wheat germ banana muffins

1 1/4 cups	all-purpose flour	300 mL
1/2 cup	natural bran	125 mL
1/3 cup	wheat germ	75 mL
1 tsp	baking powder	5 mL
1 tsp	baking soda	5 mL
Pinch	salt	Pinch
1/2 cup	butter *or* margarine	125 mL
1/2 cup	lightly packed brown sugar	125 mL
1	egg	1
2/3 cup	mashed bananas	150 mL
1/2 cup	buttermilk *or* sour milk	125 mL
1 tbsp	molasses	15 mL
3/4 cup	raisins	175 mL
1/3 cup	chopped nuts	75 mL

Preheat oven to 375° F (190° C)
12-cup muffin tin, greased or paper-lined

1. In a bowl combine flour, bran, wheat germ, baking powder, baking soda and salt; blend well.

2. In another bowl cream together butter, brown sugar and egg. Add bananas, buttermilk and molasses; mix well. Add to flour mixture; stir just until blended. Add raisins and nuts.

3. Spoon batter into prepared muffin tin, filling to top. Bake in preheated oven for 20 to 25 minutes.

simplified blueberry muffins

1	egg	1
	Milk	
1 1/2 cups	self-rising flour	375 mL
1/2 cup	granulated sugar	125 mL
1/4 cup	softened butter or margarine	50 mL
1 cup	fresh or frozen blueberries, partially thawed	250 mL

Preheat oven to 400° F (200° C)
12-cup muffin tin, greased

1. In a measuring cup combine egg and enough milk to make 1 cup (250 mL).

2. In a bowl combine flour and sugar. With a pastry blender cut in butter until crumbly. Add egg mixture; stir just until moist. Fold in blueberries.

3. Spoon batter into prepared muffin tin, filling three-quarters full. Bake in preheated oven for 20 to 25 minutes or until golden brown.

blueberry almond muffins

Preheat oven to 400° F (200° C)
Muffin tin, greased or paper-lined

2 cups	all-purpose flour	500 mL
1 cup	granulated sugar	250 mL
2 tsp	baking powder	10 mL
1/2 tsp	salt	2 mL
2	eggs	2
1/2 cup	milk	125 mL
1/3 cup	melted butter or margarine	75 mL
1 tsp	grated lemon zest	5 mL
1 tsp	lemon juice	5 mL
1	pkg (10 oz [300 g]) frozen unsweetened blueberries, divided	1

TOPPING

| 2 tbsp | granulated sugar | 25 mL |
| 1/4 cup | sliced almonds | 50 mL |

1. In a bowl combine flour, sugar, baking powder, salt, eggs, milk, butter, lemon zest and lemon juice. Blend on low speed just until moist. Beat on medium speed for 2 minutes. Add 1 cup (250 mL) blueberries; stir well.

2. Spoon batter into prepared muffin tin, filling two-thirds full. Sprinkle with remaining blueberries, sugar and almonds. Bake in preheated oven for 20 to 25 minutes or until golden brown.

grandma's blueberry gems

Preheat oven to 400° F (200° C)
Muffin tin, greased or paper-lined

2 1/4 cups	all-purpose flour	550 mL
3/4 cup	granulated sugar	175 mL
3 tsp	baking powder	15 mL
3/4 tsp	salt	4 mL
6 tbsp	butter or margarine	90 mL
3/4 cup	milk	175 mL
3/4 cup	water	175 mL
2	small eggs	2
	Grated zest of 1 lemon	
	Juice of 1/2 lemon	
1 1/2 cups	frozen blueberries, not thawed	375 mL

1. In a bowl sift together flour, sugar, baking powder and salt. Add butter, milk, water, eggs, lemon zest and lemon juice; blend well. Using a spatula, fold in blueberries.

2. Spoon batter into prepared muffin tin, filling three-quarters full or to the top. Bake in preheated oven for 25 minutes or until golden brown.

blueberry lemon muffins

1 cup	fresh blueberries *or* frozen blueberries, thawed	250 mL
2 cups	all-purpose flour	500 mL
3 tsp	baking powder	15 mL
1/2 tsp	salt	2 mL
1/4 tsp	nutmeg	1 mL
3/4 cup	granulated sugar	175 mL
	Grated zest of 1 lemon	
1	egg	1
1/4 cup	vegetable oil	50 mL
1 1/4 cups	milk	300 mL
1/2 cup	chopped walnuts	125 mL

Preheat oven to 425° F (220° C)
Muffin tin, greased or paper-lined

1. In a bowl combine blueberries and 2 tbsp (25 mL) flour: toss until lightly coated. Set aside.

2. In another bowl combine remaining flour, baking powder, salt, nutmeg and sugar; stir with a fork until well blended. Sprinkle with lemon zest.

3. In another bowl beat together egg, oil and milk. Add to flour mixture; stir just until moist and blended. Add walnuts and berries; blend well.

4. Spoon batter into prepared muffin tin, filling three-quarters full. Bake in preheated oven for 20 minutes.

muffin stuff
If using frozen berries, thaw and gently pat dry on paper towels.

variation
You can make a loaf with this batter. Spoon into a greased loaf pan. Bake at 350° F (180° C) for about 1 hour and 10 minutes.

glazed blueberry orange muffins

1 1/2 cups	all-purpose flour	375 mL
1 cup	whole wheat flour	250 mL
1 tbsp	baking powder	15 mL
1 tsp	cinnamon	5 mL
1/2 tsp	salt	2 mL
1	egg	1
1 1/4 cups	milk	300 mL
1/3 cup	vegetable oil	75 mL
1/3 cup	liquid honey *or* maple syrup	75 mL
1 tsp	grated orange zest	5 mL
1 1/2 cups	fresh blueberries *or* frozen blueberries, not thawed	375 mL
GLAZE		
1/2 cup	icing sugar	125 mL
2 to 3 tsp	orange juice	10 to 15 mL
1 tsp	grated orange zest	5 mL

Preheat oven to 400° F (200° C)
12-cup muffin tin, greased or paper-lined

1. In a bowl combine all-purpose flour, whole wheat flour, baking powder, cinnamon and salt.

2. In another bowl combine egg, milk, oil, honey and orange zest. Add to dry ingredients; stir just until blended. Do not overmix. Fold in blueberries.

3. Spoon batter into prepared muffin tin, filling to the top. Bake in preheated oven for about 20 minutes or until golden brown.

4. In a bowl combine icing sugar, orange juice and orange zest; mix until smooth. Spread over warm muffins.

muffin stuff

Omit the glaze if you are freezing the muffins.

STRAWBERRY TEA MUFFINS (PAGE 145) ➤

blueberry muffins with crunchy pecan topping

Preheat oven to 400° F (200° C)
Muffin tin, paper-lined

TOPPING

1/2 cup	chopped pecans	125 mL
2/3 cup	packed brown sugar	150 mL
2 tbsp	all-purpose flour	25 mL
1/2 tsp	cinnamon	2 mL
2 tbsp	melted butter	25 mL

1/2 cup	butter	125 mL
1 cup	granulated sugar	250 mL
1 tsp	vanilla	5 mL
3	eggs	3
2 cups	all-purpose flour	500 mL
1/2 tsp	salt	2 mL
1 tsp	baking powder	5 mL
1 tsp	baking soda	5 mL
1 1/4 cups	sour cream	300 mL
2 cups	frozen blueberries, thawed and patted dry	500 mL

1. In a bowl combine pecans, brown sugar, flour and cinnamon; mix well. Add melted butter; stir. Set aside.

2. In a bowl combine butter and sugar; cream until light and fluffy. Add vanilla; continue to beat. Add eggs one at a time; beat well.

3. In another bowl combine flour, salt, baking powder and baking soda. Add one-third of this mixture to creamed mixture; mix well. Add half sour cream and one-third flour mixture; blend well. Add remaining sour cream and remaining flour mixture; mix well.

4. Spoon batter into prepared muffin tin, filling half full. Add blueberries; top with remaining batter. Sprinkle with topping. Bake in preheated oven for 20 to 25 minutes.

◄ CHILI-PEPPER CORN MUFFINS (PAGE 158)

blueberry sour cream muffins

1 cup	fresh or frozen blueberries	250 mL
2 tbsp	all-purpose flour	25 mL
1/4 cup	butter *or* margarine	50 mL
3/4 cup	granulated sugar	175 mL
2	eggs	2
1 1/4 cups	all-purpose flour	300 mL
1/2 tsp	baking soda	2 mL
1/4 tsp	salt	1 mL
3/4 cup	sour cream	175 mL
1/2 tsp	vanilla	2 mL

Preheat oven to 450° F (230° C)
Muffin tin, greased or paper-lined

1. In a bowl combine blueberries and flour; toss to coat well. Set aside.

2. In a bowl combine butter and sugar; cream until light. Add eggs one at a time; beat well.

3. In another bowl sift together flour, baking soda and salt. Add to creamed mixture alternately with sour cream; mix well. Add blueberries and vanilla.

4. Spoon batter into prepared muffin tin, filling three-quarters full. Bake in preheated oven for about 15 minutes.

black cherry muffins

2 cups	all-purpose flour	500 mL
1 tbsp	baking powder	15 mL
1/4 tsp	salt	1 mL
1 cup	coarsely chopped pitted black cherries	250 mL
6 tbsp	softened butter or margarine	90 mL
2/3 cup	granulated sugar	150 mL
2	eggs	2
1 tsp	vanilla	5 mL
1/2 cup	milk	125 mL

Preheat oven to 400° F (200° C)
12-cup muffin tin, greased or paper-lined

1. In a bowl combine flour, baking powder and salt. In another bowl combine 1 tbsp (15 mL) flour mixture and cherries; toss well. Set aside.

2. In another bowl combine butter and sugar; beat until light and fluffy. Add eggs and vanilla; beat for 3 minutes. Add remaining flour mixture alternately with milk; beat well. Add cherries.

3. Spoon batter into prepared muffin tin, filling three-quarters full. Bake in preheated oven for 20 to 25 minutes or until golden.

marmalade muffins

	Peel of 1 grapefruit, chopped	
	Peel of 1 orange, chopped	
1 1/2 cups	buttermilk	375 mL
1 cup	granulated sugar	250 mL
1 tsp	salt	5 mL
1/2 cup	margarine	125 mL
1 3/4 cups	all-purpose flour	425 mL
2 tsp	baking powder	10 mL
1/2 tsp	baking soda	2 mL

Preheat oven to 375° F (190° C)
Muffin tin, greased or paper-lined

1. In a food processor or blender combine grapefruit peel, orange peel and buttermilk; process until finely ground. Add sugar, salt and margarine; process.

2. In a bowl combine flour, baking powder and baking soda. Add peel mixture; stir just until moist.

3. Spoon batter into prepared muffin tin, dividing evenly. Bake in preheated oven for 20 minutes.

orange surprise muffins

3 tbsp	shortening	45 mL
2 cups	all-purpose flour	500 mL
1 tbsp	baking powder	15 mL
1/2 tsp	salt	2 mL
3/4 cup	milk	175 mL
1	egg	1
1/2 cup	orange marmalade	125 mL
3 tbsp	granulated sugar	45 mL

Preheat oven to 400° F (200° C)
Muffin tin, greased

1. In a saucepan heat shortening over medium-high heat. Set aside to cool.

2. In a bowl sift together flour, baking powder and salt.

3. In a blender or food processor combine milk, egg, marmalade and sugar. Add cooled shortening; blend until thoroughly mixed.

4. Make a well in the center of dry ingredients. Add marmalade mixture; stir quickly just until moist.

5. Spoon batter into prepared muffin tin, filling two-thirds full. Bake in preheated oven for 30 to 35 minutes or until golden brown.

quick lemon muffins

6 tbsp	butter	90 mL
1 cup	granulated sugar	250 mL
2	eggs	2
1 1/2 cups	all-purpose flour	375 mL
1/2 cup	milk	125 mL
	Grated zest of 1 1/2 lemons	
1/4 tsp	salt	1 mL
1 1/2 tsp	baking powder	7 mL
TOPPING		
	Juice of 1 1/2 lemons	
1/3 cup	granulated sugar	75 mL

Preheat oven to 400° F (200° C)
Muffin tin, greased

1. In a bowl cream together butter, sugar and eggs. Add flour, milk, lemon zest, salt and baking powder; mix well.

2. Spoon batter into prepared muffin tin, filling three-quarters full. Bake in preheated oven for 15 to 20 minutes.

3. Meanwhile in a bowl combine lemon juice and sugar. When muffins are done, prick tops with a fork. Drizzle with topping.

lemon poppyseed muffins

1 cup	lemonade	250 mL
1/2 tsp	grated lemon zest	2 mL
1/4 cup	poppy seeds	50 mL
1/4 cup	butter	50 mL
1/4 cup	granulated sugar	50 mL
1	egg	1
1 tsp	vanilla	5 mL
2 cups	all-purpose flour	500 mL
1 tbsp	baking powder	15 mL
1 tsp	salt	5 mL
GLAZE		
2 tbsp	freshly squeezed lemon juice	25 mL
2 tsp	granulated sugar	10 mL

Preheat oven to 375° F (190° C)
Muffin tin, greased

1. In a saucepan heat lemonade over medium-high heat. When just about to boil, remove from heat. Add lemon zest and poppy seeds. Set aside to cool.

2. In a bowl combine butter and sugar; beat well. Add egg and vanilla; mix thoroughly.

3. In another bowl combine flour, baking powder and salt. Add to butter mixture; mix well. Add lemonade mixture; stir to moisten thoroughly.

4. Spoon batter into prepared muffin tin, filling three-quarters full. Bake in preheated oven for 20 to 25 minutes or until golden brown.

5. In a saucepan over medium-high heat, combine lemon juice and sugar. Heat, stirring constantly, just until sugar has completely dissolved. Tunnel the surface of each muffin; drizzle with glaze.

raisin lemon muffins

1 1/2 cups	all-purpose flour	375 mL
1 tbsp	baking powder	15 mL
1/2 tsp	salt	2 mL
1/4 tsp	nutmeg	1 mL
3/4 cup	brown sugar	175 mL
1 cup	rolled oats	250 mL
	Finely grated zest of 1 lemon	
1	egg	1
1/4 cup	vegetable oil	50 mL
1 cup	milk	250 mL
1/2 cup	raisins	125 mL

Preheat oven to 400° F (200° C)
12-cup muffin tin, greased or paper-lined

1. In a bowl combine flour, baking powder, salt, nutmeg and brown sugar; mix well. Add oats and lemon zest. Make a well in the center.

2. In another bowl whisk together egg, oil and milk. Add to dry ingredients; stir just until moist. Fold in raisins.

3. Spoon batter into prepared muffin tin, filling three-quarters full. Bake in preheated oven for 15 to 20 minutes.

lemon yogurt muffins

1 3/4 cups	all-purpose flour	425 mL
3/4 cup	granulated sugar	175 mL
	Grated zest of 1 large lemon	
1 tsp	baking powder	5 mL
3/4 tsp	baking soda	4 mL
1/4 tsp	salt	1 mL
8 oz	lemon yogurt	250 g
6 tbsp	melted butter, cooled	90 mL
1	egg	1
1 to 2 tbsp	fresh lemon juice	15 to 25 mL

Preheat oven to 400° F (200° C)
12-cup muffin tin, greased

1. In a bowl combine flour, sugar, lemon zest, baking powder, baking soda and salt.

2. In another bowl whisk together lemon yogurt, butter, egg and lemon juice. Add to flour mixture; stir just until blended.

3. Spoon batter into prepared muffin tin, dividing evenly. Bake in preheated oven for 20 to 25 minutes.

great lemonade muffins

1 3/4 cups	sifted all-purpose flour	425 mL
1/4 cup	granulated sugar	50 mL
2 1/2 tsp	baking powder	12 mL
3/4 tsp	salt	4 mL
1	egg, well-beaten	1
1	can (6 oz [175 g]) frozen lemonade concentrate, thawed	1
1/4 cup	milk	50 mL
1/3 cup	cooking oil	75 mL
1/2 cup	chopped walnuts	125 mL
	Granulated sugar	

Preheat oven to 400° F (200° C)
12-cup muffin tin, greased or paper-lined

1. In a bowl sift together flour, sugar, baking powder and salt. Make a well in the center.

2. In another bowl combine egg, 1/2 cup (125 mL) lemonade, milk and oil. Add to flour mixture quickly; stir just until moist and blended. Add walnuts; stir gently.

3. Spoon batter into prepared muffin tin, dividing evenly. Bake in preheated oven for 25 minutes. Remove from tins. While still hot brush muffins with remaining lemonade; sprinkle with sugar.

orange muffins

2	oranges, cut into 8 pieces	2
1/2 cup	orange juice	125 mL
1/2 cup	dates or raisins	125 mL
1	egg	1
1/2 cup	margarine	125 mL
1/4 cup	wheat germ or bran	50 mL
1 1/2 cups	all-purpose flour	375 mL
1 tsp	baking powder	5 mL
1 tsp	baking soda	5 mL
3/4 cup	granulated sugar	175 mL
Pinch	salt	Pinch

Preheat oven to 400° F (200° C)
Muffin tin, greased or paper-lined

1. In a blender or food processor, combine oranges, orange juice, dates, egg and margarine; process until well blended. Scrape down edges of blender. Add wheat germ; process again.

2. In a bowl sift together flour, baking powder, baking soda, sugar and salt. Add orange mixture; blend well.

3. Spoon batter into prepared muffin tin, dividing evenly. Bake in preheated oven for about 15 minutes.

orangeberry muffins

1	medium-sized orange, cut into pieces	1
1/3 cup	shortening	75 mL
1	egg	1
1/2 cup	milk	125 mL
1 1/2 cups	all-purpose flour	375 mL
3/4 cup	granulated sugar	175 mL
2 tsp	baking powder	10 mL
1 tsp	baking soda	5 mL
1 cup	fresh or frozen blueberries	250 mL

Preheat oven to 375° F (190° C)
12-cup muffin tin, greased

1. In a blender or food processor combine orange pieces, shortening, egg and milk. Blend until orange is finely chopped. Set aside.

2. In a bowl combine flour, sugar, baking powder and baking soda. Make a well in the center. Add orange mixture; stir just until moist and blended. Fold in blueberries.

3. Spoon batter into prepared muffin tin, dividing evenly. Bake in preheated oven for 22 to 25 minutes or until golden brown.

orange chocolate chip muffins

1	egg	1
1 cup	milk	250 mL
1/2 cup	melted margarine	125 mL
1/2 tsp	grated orange zest	2 mL
1/4 cup	orange juice	50 mL
1 1/2 cups	all-purpose flour	375 mL
1 cup	whole wheat flour	250 mL
1/2 cup	granulated sugar	125 mL
1 tbsp	baking powder	15 mL
1/2 tsp	salt	2 mL
1/2 cup	semi-sweet chocolate chips	125 mL

Preheat oven to 400° F (200° C)
12-cup muffin tin, greased or paper-lined

1. In a bowl beat egg with a fork. Add milk, margarine, orange zest and orange juice.

2. In another bowl combine all-purpose flour, whole wheat flour, sugar, baking powder and salt. Add egg mixture; stir just until moist. Fold in chocolate chips.

3. Spoon batter into prepared muffin tin, filling to the top. Bake in preheated oven for about 20 minutes.

cinnamon nut orange muffins

1 1/2 cups	all-purpose flour	375 mL
1 1/2 tsp	baking powder	7 mL
1/4 tsp	salt	1 mL
1/4 tsp	nutmeg	1 mL
1/4 cup	pecans	50 mL
1/3 cup	butter	75 mL
1/2 cup	granulated sugar	125 mL
1	egg	1
1/2 tsp	vanilla	2 mL
1 tsp	orange zest	5 mL
1/2 cup	milk	125 mL
CINNAMON TOPPING		
1/4 cup	melted butter	50 mL
1/2 cup	granulated sugar	125 mL
1 tsp	cinnamon	5 mL

Preheat oven to 375° F (190° C)
Muffin tin, greased

1. In a bowl combine flour, baking powder, salt, nutmeg and pecans.

2. In another bowl cream together butter and sugar. Beat in egg, vanilla and orange zest; blend well. Add flour mixture alternately with milk, stirring just until blended.

3. Spoon batter into prepared muffin tin, filling three-quarters full. Bake in preheated oven for 20 to 25 minutes.

4. Remove muffins from tins. While still hot dip tops in butter; roll in sugar and cinnamon.

orange date muffins

1 1/4 cups	whole wheat flour	300 mL
1 cup	all-purpose flour	250 mL
3/4 cup	lightly packed brown sugar	175 mL
2 tsp	baking powder	10 mL
1 tsp	baking soda	5 mL
1/2 tsp	salt	2 mL
3/4 cup	chopped dates	175 mL
1 tsp	grated orange zest	5 mL
2	eggs	2
1/2 cup	orange juice	125 mL
1/3 cup	melted butter	75 mL

Preheat oven to 400° F (200° C)
12-cup muffin tin, paper-lined

1. In a bowl combine whole wheat flour, all-purpose flour, brown sugar, baking powder, baking soda and salt; mix well. Add dates and orange zest.

2. In another bowl beat eggs. Add orange juice and butter; blend well. Add to dry ingredients; stir with a fork just until moist.

3. Spoon batter into prepared muffin tin, dividing evenly. Bake in preheated oven for 15 to 20 minutes.

mandarin orange muffins

Preheat oven to 400° F (200° C)
12-cup muffin tin, paper-lined

1 1/2 cups	all-purpose flour	375 mL
1/2 cup	granulated sugar	125 mL
2 1/2 tsp	baking powder	12 mL
1/4 tsp	salt	1 mL
1/4 tsp	allspice	1 mL
1/2 tsp	nutmeg	2 mL
1	egg	1
3/4 cup	milk	175 mL
1/3 cup	melted butter	75 mL
1 cup	mandarin orange segments, each cut into 4 pieces	250 mL
2 tbsp	granulated sugar	25 mL

1. In a bowl sift together flour, sugar, baking powder, salt, allspice and nutmeg.

2. In another bowl beat egg. Add milk and melted butter; blend well. Add to flour mixture; stir just until moist. Add orange pieces; stir gently.

3. Spoon batter into prepared muffin tin, dividing evenly. Sprinkle with sugar. Bake in preheated oven for about 20 minutes.

pineapple orange muffins

Preheat oven to 400° F (200° C)
Muffin tin, greased or paper-lined

2 cups	all-purpose flour	500 mL
1/2 tsp	salt	2 mL
4 tsp	baking powder	20 mL
1/4 cup	granulated sugar	50 mL
1	egg	1
1 cup	unsweetened pineapple juice	250 mL
1/4 cup	melted shortening	50 mL
1/2 cup	well-drained crushed pineapple	125 mL

TOPPING

2 tbsp	granulated sugar	25 mL
1 tsp	grated orange zest	5 mL

1. In a bowl sift together flour, salt, baking powder and sugar.

2. In another bowl beat together egg and pineapple juice. Add shortening; blend well. Add to flour mixture; stir just until moist and blended. Fold in pineapple.

3. In a bowl combine sugar and orange zest.

4. Spoon batter into prepared muffin tin, filling two-thirds full. Sprinkle with topping. Bake in preheated oven for 25 minutes.

old-fashioned orange tea cakes

2 cups	sifted cake flour	500 mL
2 tsp	baking powder	10 mL
2 tbsp	butter *or* shortening	25 mL
1 cup	granulated sugar	250 mL
1	egg	1
1 tbsp	grated orange zest	15 mL
1/4 cup	milk	50 mL
1/2 cup	orange juice	125 mL

Preheat oven to 350° F (180° C)
Muffin tin, paper-lined

1. In a bowl combine flour and baking powder.

2. In another bowl cream together butter and sugar. Add egg; beat until light and fluffy. Add orange zest; blend well. Add flour mixture alternately with milk and orange juice; beat until smooth.

3. Spoon batter into prepared muffin tin, filling two-thirds full. Bake in preheated oven for 25 minutes.

peaches n' cream muffins

2	eggs	2
1 1/4 cups	milk	300 mL
1/3 cup	liquid honey	75 mL
1/4 cup	melted margarine	50 mL
1 tsp	grated lemon zest	5 mL
1 1/2 cups	all-bran cereal	375 mL
2 cups	all-purpose flour	500 mL
1 tbsp	baking powder	15 mL
1 tsp	cinnamon	5 mL
1/2 tsp	salt	2 mL
1	can (14 oz [398 mL]) sliced peaches, drained and cut into cubes	1
4 oz	cream cheese, cut into cubes	125 g

Preheat oven to 400° F (200° C)
12-cup muffin tin, greased or paper-lined

1. In a bowl beat eggs lightly. Add milk, honey, margarine, lemon zest and cereal; stir well.

2. In another bowl combine flour, baking powder, cinnamon and salt. Add cereal mixture; stir just until blended. Fold in peaches and cheese.

3. Spoon batter into prepared muffin tin, dividing evenly. Bake in preheated oven for 20 to 25 minutes or until golden brown.

peach melba dessert muffins

1 cup	diced peaches	250 mL
1/2 tsp	cinnamon	2 mL
2 cups	all-purpose flour	500 mL
1/2 cup	granulated sugar	125 mL
2 1/2 tsp	baking powder	12 mL
1/2 tsp	salt	2 mL
1/2 cup	chopped walnuts	125 mL
1	egg	1
1 cup	milk	250 mL
1/3 cup	melted butter or margarine	75 mL
2 tbsp	brandy	25 mL
	Raspberry jam	

Preheat oven to 400° F (200° C)
12-cup muffin tin, greased or paper-lined

1. In a bowl combine peaches and cinnamon. Set aside.

2. In a bowl sift together flour, sugar, baking powder and salt. Add walnuts; blend well. Make a well in the center.

3. In another bowl whisk together egg, milk, butter and brandy. Add peach mixture; blend well. Add to dry ingredients; stir just until moist.

4. Spoon batter into prepared muffin tin, filling half full. Add about 1 tsp (5 mL) raspberry jam; cover with remaining batter. Bake in preheated oven for 20 to 25 minutes.

special pear cheese muffins

2 cups	all-purpose flour	500 mL
1/3 cup	granulated sugar	75 mL
1 tbsp	baking powder	15 mL
1/2 tsp	salt	2 mL
1/4 tsp	pumpkin pie spice	1 mL
1 cup	shredded Colby cheese	250 mL
2	medium-sized pears, peeled and cut into large chunks	2
1 cup	milk	250 mL
2	eggs	2
1/4 cup	melted butter	50 mL

Preheat oven to 425° F (220° C)
15-cup muffin tin, paper-lined

1. In a bowl combine flour, sugar, baking powder, salt and spice. Make a well in the center.

2. In a blender or food processor combine cheese, pears, milk, eggs and butter; process until pears are finely chopped. Add to flour mixture; stir just until moist and blended.

3. Spoon batter into prepared muffin tin, filling three-quarters full. Bake in preheated oven for 20 to 25 minutes.

pineapple muffins

2 cups	all-purpose flour	500 mL
1/2 cup	granulated sugar	125 mL
3 tsp	baking powder	15 mL
1/2 tsp	salt	2 mL
1	egg	1
1/4 cup	cooking oil	50 mL
1 cup	milk	250 mL
1/2 cup	well-drained crushed pineapple	125 mL

Preheat oven to 400° F (200° C)
18-cup muffin tin, greased

1. In a bowl combine flour, sugar, baking powder and salt. Make a well in the center.

2. In another bowl beat egg. Add oil, milk and pineapple; mix well. Add to dry ingredients; stir just until moist.

3. Spoon batter into prepared muffin tin, dividing evenly. Bake in preheated oven for 20 to 25 minutes.

pineapple coconut delights

1 1/2 cups	all-purpose flour	375 mL
1 tsp	baking powder	5 mL
1/2 tsp	baking soda	2 mL
1/2 tsp	salt	2 mL
1/4 cup	softened butter	50 mL
1/2 cup	granulated sugar	125 mL
1	egg	1
1 cup	sour cream	250 mL
1 tsp	rum extract	5 mL
1 cup	drained crushed pineapple	250 mL
1/2 cup	flaked coconut	125 mL

Preheat oven to 375° F (190° C)
12-cup muffin tin, greased or paper-lined

1. In a bowl combine flour, baking powder, baking soda and salt.

2. In another bowl beat together butter, sugar, egg, sour cream and rum. Add to flour mixture; stir just until blended. Add pineapple and coconut.

3. Spoon batter into prepared muffin tin, filling three-quarters full. Bake in preheated oven for 20 to 25 minutes.

pineapple upside-down muffins

1/4 cup	melted butter	50 mL
1/3 cup	brown sugar	75 mL
8 oz	drained crushed pineapple	250 g
1 1/2 cups	all-purpose flour	375 mL
1/2 cup	granulated sugar	125 mL
1/4 tsp	salt	1 mL
1/2 tsp	baking soda	2 mL
1 tsp	baking powder	5 mL
1 tsp	cinnamon	5 mL
2	eggs, beaten	2
1 cup	buttermilk	250 mL
2 tbsp	melted butter	25 mL

Preheat oven to 375° F (190° C)
12-cup muffin tin, greased

1. Spoon melted butter evenly into prepared muffin tin. Sprinkle brown sugar over top. Spoon pineapple over brown sugar. Set aside.

2. In a bowl combine flour, sugar, salt, baking soda, baking powder and cinnamon. Make a well in the center.

3. In another bowl whisk together eggs, buttermilk and butter. Add quickly to flour mixture; stir just until moist and blended.

4. Spoon batter into muffin cups over pineapple. Bake in preheated oven for 20 to 25 minutes.

5. When cool, remove muffins from pan. Serve pineapple-side up.

tropical treat muffins

2 cups	all-purpose flour	500 mL
2 tsp	baking powder	10 mL
1/2 tsp	baking soda	2 mL
1/2 tsp	salt	2 mL
1/2 cup	brown sugar	125 mL
1	egg, well-beaten	1
1 cup	sour cream	250 mL
1	can (8 oz [250 g]) crushed pineapple, with juice	1
1/3 cup	oil *or* melted shortening	75 mL
1/2 cup	chopped pecans	125 mL

Preheat oven to 400° F (200° C)
18-cup muffin tin, greased

1. In a bowl sift together flour, baking powder, baking soda and salt. Add brown sugar.

2. In another bowl combine egg and sour cream; mix well. Add pineapple (with juice), oil and pecans. Add to flour mixture; stir just until moist.

3. Spoon batter into prepared muffin tin, dividing evenly. Bake in preheated oven for 20 minutes.

favorite raspberry muffins

1 1/2 cups	all-purpose flour	375 mL
1/2 cup	quick-cooking rolled oats *or* oatmeal	125 mL
1/2 cup	packed brown sugar	125 mL
1/4 tsp	salt	1 mL
2 tsp	baking powder	10 mL
1 tsp	baking soda	5 mL
1 cup	frozen raspberries, not thawed	250 mL
2	eggs	2
1/2 cup	buttermilk	125 mL
1/2 cup	melted margarine	125 mL

TOPPING

1/4 cup	softened butter	50 mL
1/4 cup	brown sugar	50 mL
1/4 cup	quick-cooking rolled oats *or* oatmeal	50 mL
1/4 cup	all-purpose flour	50 mL
1 tsp	cinnamon	5 mL

Preheat oven to 400° F (200° C)
Muffin tin, greased or paper-lined

1. In a bowl combine flour, oats, brown sugar, salt, baking powder and baking soda. Add frozen raspberries; blend well.

2. In another bowl whisk together eggs, buttermilk and margarine. Add to flour mixture; stir just until moist and blended.

3. In a bowl cream together butter and brown sugar. Add oats, flour and cinnamon; mix well.

4. Spoon batter into prepared muffin tin, filling two-thirds full. Spoon topping over muffins evenly. Bake in preheated oven for 15 to 20 minutes.

raspberry almond muffins

1/2 cup	butter (room temperature)	125 mL
3/4 cup	granulated sugar	175 mL
2	eggs	2
1 tsp	baking powder	5 mL
1/2 tsp	baking soda	2 mL
1 tsp	almond extract	5 mL
2 cups	all-purpose flour	500 mL
1 cup	plain yogurt *or* buttermilk	250 mL
1/4 cup	raspberry preserves	50 mL
5 oz	almond paste	150 g

Preheat oven to 350° F (180° C)
Muffin tin, paper-lined

1. In a bowl combine butter and sugar; cream until light and fluffy. Beat in eggs one at a time. Add baking powder, baking soda and almond extract; mix well. Fold in 1 cup (250 mL) flour. Add yogurt and remaining flour; mix well.

2. Spoon batter into prepared muffin tin, filling half full. Top each with 1 tsp (5 mL) raspberry preserves and piece of almond paste. Top with remaining batter. Bake in preheated oven for 25 to 30 minutes or until lightly browned.

raspberry-blueberry-cornmeal muffins

1 cup	yellow cornmeal	250 mL
1 cup	all-purpose flour	250 mL
1/3 cup	granulated sugar	75 mL
2 tsp	baking powder	10 mL
1/4 tsp	salt	1 mL
1 cup	buttermilk	250 mL
6 tbsp	melted butter	90 mL
1	egg, slightly beaten	1
1 cup	fresh or frozen blueberries	250 mL
1/2 cup	fresh or frozen raspberries	125 mL

Preheat oven to 400° F (200° C)
Muffin tin, greased or paper-lined

1. In a bowl sift together cornmeal, flour, sugar, baking powder and salt. Make a well in the center.

2. In another bowl combine buttermilk, butter and egg. Add to dry ingredients; stir just until moist and blended. Fold in blueberries and raspberries.

3. Spoon batter into prepared muffin tin, filling three-quarters full. Bake in preheated oven for 20 to 25 minutes or until golden brown.

raspberry pecan streusel muffins

Preheat oven to 375° F (190° C)
12-cup muffin tin, greased

PECAN STREUSEL TOPPING

1/4 cup	chopped pecans	50 mL
1/4 cup	packed brown sugar	50 mL
1/4 cup	all-purpose flour	50 mL
2 tbsp	butter or margarine, melted	25 mL

1 1/2 cups	all-purpose flour	375 mL
1/2 cup	granulated sugar	125 mL
2 tsp	baking powder	10 mL
1/2 cup	milk	125 mL
1/2 cup	melted butter or margarine	125 mL
1	egg, beaten	1
1 cup	fresh or frozen raspberries, unsweetened	250 mL

1. In a bowl combine pecans, brown sugar and flour. Add butter; mix until crumbly. Set aside.

2. In a bowl combine flour, sugar and baking powder. Make a well in the center.

3. In another bowl combine milk, butter and egg; mix well. Add to flour mixture; stir just until moist.

4. Spoon batter into prepared muffin tin, filling half full. Add a few raspberries. Top with remaining batter. Sprinkle with streusel topping. Bake in preheated oven for 25 to 30 minutes or until browned.

best ever rhubarb pecan muffins

Preheat oven to 350° F (180° C)
12-cup muffin tin, lightly greased

2 cups	all-purpose flour	500 mL
3/4 cup	granulated sugar	175 mL
1 1/2 tsp	baking powder	7 mL
1/2 tsp	baking soda	2 mL
1 tsp	salt	5 mL
3/4 cup	chopped pecans	175 mL
1	egg	1
1/4 cup	vegetable oil	50 mL
2 tsp	grated orange zest	10 mL
3/4 cup	orange juice	175 mL
1 1/4 cups	finely chopped fresh rhubarb	300 mL

1. In a bowl combine flour, sugar, baking powder, baking soda, salt and pecans.

2. In another bowl beat egg. Add oil, orange zest and orange juice. Add to flour mixture; stir just until moist and blended. Add rhubarb.

3. Spoon batter into prepared muffin tin, filling to top. Bake in preheated oven for 25 to 30 minutes.

strawberry cheesecake muffins

Preheat oven to 375° F (190° C)
12-cup muffin tin, greased or paper-lined

4 oz	softened cream cheese	125 g
1/4 cup	sifted icing sugar	50 mL
2 1/2 cups	all-purpose flour	625 mL
1 tbsp	baking powder	15 mL
1/2 tsp	salt	2 mL
1	egg	1
1 1/4 cups	milk	300 mL
1/2 cup	lightly packed brown sugar	125 mL
1/3 cup	melted butter or margarine	75 mL
1 tsp	grated lemon zest	5 mL
1/4 tsp	almond extract	1 mL
1/4 cup	strawberry jam	1 mL

1. In a bowl combine cream cheese and icing sugar; beat until smooth. Set aside.

2. In a bowl combine flour, baking powder and salt.

3. In another bowl combine egg, milk, brown sugar, butter, lemon zest and almond extract. Add to flour mixture; stir just until moist and blended.

4. Spoon batter into prepared muffin tin, filling half full. Add 1 tbsp (15 mL) cream cheese mixture and 1 tsp (5 mL) jam. Top with remaining batter. Bake in preheated oven for about 20 minutes or until lightly browned.

variation
You can use any type of jam such as apricot, peach, grape, etc.

strawberry tea muffins

Preheat oven to 400° F (200° C)
Muffin tin, greased or paper-lined

1 1/4 cups	all-purpose flour	300 mL
2/3 cup	oat bran	150 mL
1 1/2 tsp	baking powder	7 mL
1/2 tsp	baking soda	2 mL
1/2 cup	granulated sugar	125 mL
2	eggs	2
4 tbsp	butter, melted	50 mL
1 cup	buttermilk	250 mL
1/2 cup	strawberry preserves	125 mL
1/4 cup	sliced almonds	50 mL

1. In a bowl combine flour, oat bran, baking powder, baking soda and sugar. Make a well in the center.

2. In another bowl whisk together eggs, butter and buttermilk. Add to flour mixture; stir just until moist and blended.

3. Spoon batter into prepared muffin tin, filling half full. Add 1 heaping tbsp (15 mL) strawberry preserves. Top with remaining batter. Sprinkle with sliced almonds. Bake in preheated oven for 15 to 20 minutes or until golden brown.

vegetable muffins

applesauce carrot muffins

3 cups	all-purpose flour	750 mL
2 1/2 tsp	baking powder	12 mL
1 tsp	baking soda	5 mL
1/2 tsp	salt	2 mL
3 tsp	cinnamon	15 mL
1 tsp	ground cloves	5 mL
1/2 tsp	nutmeg	2 mL
1 1/2 cups	brown sugar	375 mL
1 cup	oil	250 mL
1 cup	applesauce	250 mL
3 cups	grated carrots	750 mL
3	eggs, slightly beaten	3

Preheat oven to 400° F (200° C)
Muffin tin, greased or paper-lined

1. In a bowl sift together flour, baking powder, baking soda, salt, cinnamon, cloves and nutmeg. Add brown sugar, oil, applesauce, carrots and eggs; mix well.

2. Spoon batter into prepared muffin tin, filling three-quarters full. Bake in preheated oven for 18 to 20 minutes.

carrot cake muffins

1 cup	all-purpose flour	250 mL
3/4 cup	quick-cooking rolled oats	175 mL
1 1/2 tsp	baking powder	7 mL
1 tsp	baking soda	5 mL
1 tsp	cinnamon	5 mL
3/4 cup	raisins *or* chopped dates	175 mL
1	egg, beaten	1
1 1/4 cups	sweetened condensed skim milk	300 mL
1 1/2 cups	grated carrots	375 mL
1/2 cup	drained crushed pineapple	125 mL
2 tbsp	vegetable oil	25 mL
2 tsp	grated orange zest	10 mL

Preheat oven to 375° F (190° C)
Muffin tin, greased or paper-lined

1. In a bowl combine flour, oats, baking powder, baking soda, cinnamon and raisins.

2. In another bowl combine egg, milk, carrots, pineapple, oil and orange zest. Add to dry ingredients; stir just until blended.

3. Spoon batter into prepared muffin tin, filling three-quarters full. Bake in preheated oven for 20 to 25 minutes or until toothpick inserted in center comes out clean and dry.

coconut pecan carrot muffins

2 1/4 cups	all-purpose flour	550 mL
2/3 cup	brown sugar	150 mL
1/2 cup	shredded coconut	125 mL
1/2 cup	pecans	125 mL
1/2 cup	raisins	125 mL
1 tbsp	baking powder	15 mL
1 tsp	salt	5 mL
1 tsp	cinnamon	5 mL
1 1/2 cups	grated carrots	375 mL
2/3 cup	milk	150 mL
1/4 cup	vegetable oil	50 mL
1 tsp	vanilla	5 mL
1	egg	1

Preheat oven to 375° F (190° C)
12-cup muffin tin, greased or paper-lined

1. In a bowl combine flour, brown sugar, coconut, pecans, raisins, baking powder, salt and cinnamon. Add carrots.

2. In another bowl combine milk, oil, vanilla and egg. Add to flour mixture; stir just until moist.

3. Spoon batter into prepared muffin tin, dividing evenly. Bake in preheated oven for 40 to 45 minutes.

corn carrot muffins

1 cup	shredded raw carrots	250 mL
1 cup	yellow cornmeal	250 mL
1 cup	milk	250 mL
2	eggs, slightly beaten	2
2 tbsp	oil	25 mL
1 cup	all-purpose flour	250 mL
2 1/2 tsp	baking powder	12 mL
1 tsp	salt	5 mL

Preheat oven to 400° F (200° C)
12-cup muffin tin, greased

1. In a bowl combine carrots and cornmeal.

2. In a saucepan over medium-high heat, bring milk to a boil. Add to carrot mixture. Cool to room temperature. Add eggs and oil.

3. In another bowl combine flour, baking powder and salt. Add to carrot mixture; blend well.

4. Spoon batter into prepared muffin tin, dividing evenly. Bake in preheated oven for 20 minutes.

carrot pineapple muffins

1 1/2 cups	all-purpose flour	375 mL
2/3 cup	granulated sugar	150 mL
1 tsp	baking powder	5 mL
1 tsp	baking soda	5 mL
1/2 tsp	salt	2 mL
1 tsp	cinnamon	5 mL
Pinch	nutmeg	Pinch
2/3 cup	vegetable oil	150 mL
2	eggs	2
1 cup	grated carrots	250 mL
1 tsp	vanilla	5 mL
1/2 cup	crushed pineapple, with juice	125 mL

Preheat oven to 350° F (180° C)
12-cup muffin tin, greased

1. In a bowl whisk together flour, sugar, baking powder, baking soda, salt, cinnamon and nutmeg. Make a well in the center.

2. In another bowl combine oil, eggs, carrots, vanilla and pineapple. Add to dry mixture; stir just until blended.

3. Spoon batter into prepared muffin tin, dividing evenly. Bake in preheated oven for 25 to 30 minutes.

spicy traditional pineapple carrot muffins

1 1/4 cups	all-bran cereal	300 mL
1	can (14 oz [398 mL]) crushed pineapple, with juice	1
1/4 cup	milk	50 mL
1	egg	1
1/2 cup	packed brown sugar	125 mL
1/3 cup	oil	75 mL
1 cup	shredded carrots	250 mL
2 cups	all-purpose flour	500 mL
1 tbsp	baking powder	15 mL
2 1/2 tsp	cinnamon	12 mL
1 tsp	ginger	5 mL
1 tsp	salt	5 mL
1/2 cup	raisins	125 mL

Preheat oven to 400° F (200° C)
12-cup muffin tin, greased

1. In a bowl combine cereal, pineapple (with juice) and milk. Let stand for 5 minutes. Add egg, brown sugar, oil and carrots.

2. In another bowl combine flour, baking powder, cinnamon, ginger and salt. Add cereal mixture and raisins; stir just until moist.

3. Spoon batter into prepared muffin tin, filling to top. Bake in preheated oven for 20 to 25 minutes or until tops are firm to the touch.

pineapple walnut carrot muffins

1 1/2 cups	all-purpose flour	375 mL
1 1/2 cups	shredded carrots	375 mL
1/4 cup	granulated sugar	50 mL
3 1/2 oz	coarsely chopped walnuts	90 g
1 tsp	cinnamon	5 mL
1 tsp	baking soda	5 mL
1/4 tsp	baking powder	1 mL
1/4 tsp	salt	1 mL
1/4 tsp	nutmeg	1 mL
3	egg whites, lightly beaten	3
2 cups	drained crushed pineapple	500 mL
1/4 cup	water	50 mL
2 tbsp + 2 tsp	frozen apple juice concentrate, thawed	25 mL + 10 mL
1 tbsp + 2 tsp	vegetable oil	15 mL + 10 mL

Preheat oven to 400° F (200° C)

Muffin tin, greased or paper-lined

1. In a bowl combine flour, carrots, sugar, walnuts, cinnamon, baking soda, baking powder, salt and nutmeg.

2. In another bowl combine egg whites, pineapple, water, apple juice concentrate and oil. Add to flour mixture; mix with a fork just until blended. Do not overmix.

3. Spoon batter into prepared muffin tin, dividing evenly. Bake in preheated oven for 25 to 30 minutes.

corn muffins

1 cup	yellow cornmeal	250 mL
1 cup	all-purpose flour	250 mL
2 tbsp	granulated sugar	25 mL
4 tsp	baking powder	20 mL
1/2 tsp	salt	2 mL
1 cup	milk	250 mL
1/4 cup	shortening	50 mL
1	egg	1

Preheat oven to 425° F (220° C)
12-cup muffin tin, greased

1. In a bowl combine cornmeal, flour, sugar, baking powder, salt, milk, shortening and egg; stir until well blended.

2. Spoon batter into prepared muffin tin, filling two-thirds full. Bake in preheated oven for 15 minutes or until golden brown.

zucchini and carrot muffins

1 1/2 cups	all-purpose flour	375 mL
3/4 cup	packed brown sugar	175 mL
1 tsp	baking powder	5 mL
1/2 tsp	ginger	2 mL
1/4 tsp	baking soda	1 mL
2	eggs, slightly beaten	2
1 1/2 cups	shredded carrots	375 mL
1 cup	shredded zucchini	250 mL
1/2 cup	raisins	125 mL
1/2 cup	chopped walnuts	125 mL
1/2 cup	oil	125 mL
1/4 cup	honey	50 mL
1 tsp	vanilla	5 mL
CITRUS CREAM CHEESE FROSTING		
8 oz	light cream cheese	250 g
1/2 cup	icing sugar	125 mL
2 tbsp	orange juice	25 mL
1 tbsp	finely shredded orange or lemon zest	15 mL

Preheat oven to 375° F (190° C)
Muffin tin, paper-lined

1. In a bowl combine flour, brown sugar, baking powder, ginger and baking soda.

2. In another bowl combine eggs, carrots, zucchini, raisins, walnuts, oil, honey and vanilla. Add to flour mixture; stir just until blended.

3. Spoon batter into prepared muffin tin, filling three-quarters full. Bake in preheated oven for 15 to 20 minutes.

4. In a bowl combine cream cheese, icing sugar, orange juice and zest; beat on medium speed until fluffy. Spread over cooled muffins.

cornmeal muffins

1/2 cup	all-purpose flour	125 mL
1 tbsp	granulated sugar	15 mL
1 tbsp	baking powder	15 mL
3/4 tsp	salt	4 mL
1 1/2 cups	white cornmeal	375 mL
1/4 cup	melted butter or margarine	50 mL
1	egg, well beaten	1
1 cup	milk	250 mL

Preheat oven to 425° F (220° C)
12-cup muffin tin, greased

1. In a bowl sift together flour, sugar, baking powder and salt. Mix in cornmeal. Make a well in the center.

2. In another bowl combine butter, egg and milk. Add to flour mixture; stir until well blended. Do not overmix.

3. Spoon batter into prepared muffin tin, filling three-quarters full. Bake in preheated oven for 20 to 25 minutes or until golden brown.

muffin stuff

Most recipes call for yellow cornmeal but try this one using white cornmeal.

buttermilk cornmeal muffins

1 cup	cornmeal	250 mL
1 1/2 cups	buttermilk	375 mL
1 1/4 cups	all-purpose flour	300 mL
1 1/2 tsp	baking powder	7 mL
1 tsp	baking soda	5 mL
1 tsp	salt	5 mL
1/2 cup	granulated sugar	125 mL
1	egg	1
1/3 cup	melted butter, cooled	75 mL

Preheat oven to 400° F (200° C)
12-cup muffin tin, greased or paper-lined

1. In a bowl combine cornmeal and buttermilk. Set aside.

2. In another bowl combine flour, baking powder, baking soda, salt and sugar.

3. In another bowl whisk together egg and butter. Add cornmeal mixture; stir well. Add to flour mixture; stir just until blended. Do not overmix.

4. Spoon batter into prepared muffin tin, filling two-thirds full. Bake in preheated oven for 15 minutes.

golden cheddar corn muffins

1 cup	cornmeal	250 mL
1 cup	shredded old Cheddar cheese	250 mL
1 cup	all-purpose flour	250 mL
1/2 tsp	baking soda	2 mL
1/2 tsp	salt	2 mL
3	eggs	3
1	can (10 oz [284 mL]) corn creamed	1
1 cup	buttermilk	250 mL
1/4 cup	vegetable oil	50 mL
2 tbsp	chopped fresh parsley	25 mL

Preheat oven to 400° F (200° C)
12-cup muffin tin, well-greased

1. In a bowl combine cornmeal, cheese, flour, baking soda and salt.

2. In another bowl whisk together eggs, corn, buttermilk and oil. Add to dry ingredients; stir well. Add parsley; stir just until blended.

3. Spoon batter into prepared muffin tin, filling three-quarters full. Bake in preheated oven for 25 to 30 minutes or until tops are firm to the touch.

mexican-style corn muffins

1/2 cup + 1 tbsp	all-purpose flour	125 mL + 15 mL
1 1/2 oz	yellow cornmeal	40g
2 tsp	granulated sugar	10 mL
1 1/2 tsp	baking powder	7 mL
1/4 tsp	salt	1 mL
1/4 cup	skim milk	50 mL
1	egg, lightly beaten	1
2 tbsp	water	25 mL
1 tbsp	vegetable oil	15 mL
1/2 cup	canned Mexican-style corn, drained	125 mL
1 tbsp	chopped green chilies	15 mL

Preheat oven to 400° F (200° C)
6-cup muffin tin, paper-lined

1. In a bowl combine flour, cornmeal, sugar, baking powder and salt.

2. In another bowl combine milk, egg, water and oil. Add to flour mixture; stir to blend well. Add corn and chilies; stir just until blended.

3. Spoon batter into prepared muffin tin, dividing evenly. Bake in preheated oven for 15 to 20 minutes.

double corn pepper muffins

1 1/2 cups	all-purpose flour	375 mL
3/4 cup	cornmeal	175 mL
1/4 cup	granulated sugar	50 mL
1 tbsp	chili powder	15 mL
1/2 tsp	salt	2 mL
1/2 tsp	baking soda	2 mL
1/4 tsp	dried crushed chilies	1 mL
3	eggs	3
2/3 cup	buttermilk *or* sour milk	150 mL
2 tbsp	vegetable oil	25 mL
1 cup	frozen corn kernels, thawed *or* 1 can (12 oz [375 g]) corn niblets, drained	250 mL
1/2 cup	chopped red or green bell peppers	125 mL

Preheat oven to 375° F (190° C)
12-cup muffin tin, greased or paper-lined

1. In a bowl combine flour, cornmeal, sugar, chili powder, salt, baking soda and chilies.

2. In another bowl combine eggs, buttermilk and oil; mix well. Add corn and chopped peppers; blend well. Add to flour mixture; mix just enough to moisten.

3. Spoon batter into prepared muffin tin, dividing evenly. Bake in preheated oven for 15 to 18 minutes or until golden brown. Serve warm.

oatmeal corn muffins

1 cup	all-purpose flour	250 mL
1 tsp	baking powder	5 mL
3/4 tsp	salt	4 mL
1/2 cup	yellow cornmeal	125 mL
1/2 cup	old-fashioned oats	125 mL
1 cup	buttermilk	250 mL
1	egg	1
1/3 cup	packed light brown sugar	75 mL
1/2 cup	melted butter or margarine	125 mL

Preheat oven to 400° F (200° C)
12-cup muffin tin, greased or paper-lined

1. In a bowl combine flour, baking powder and salt.

2. In another bowl combine cornmeal, oats and buttermilk. Add egg, brown sugar and butter; beat with a spoon until well blended. Add flour mixture; stir just until blended.

3. Spoon batter into prepared muffin tin, dividing evenly. Bake in preheated oven for about 25 minutes or until golden brown.

bell pepper muffins

1/4 cup	butter *or* margarine	50 mL
1/4 cup	finely chopped red bell peppers	50 mL
1/4 cup	finely chopped yellow bell peppers	50 mL
1/4 cup	finely chopped green bell peppers	50 mL
2 cups	all-purpose flour	500 mL
2 tbsp	granulated sugar	25 mL
1 tbsp	baking powder	15 mL
3/4 tsp	salt	4 mL
1/2 tsp	dried basil leaves	2 mL
1 cup	milk	250 mL
2	eggs	2

Preheat oven to 400° F (200° C)
12-cup muffin tin, greased or paper-lined

1. In a skillet heat butter over medium-high heat. Cook red, yellow and green peppers for 3 minutes or until bright and tender-crisp. Set aside.

2. In a bowl combine flour, sugar, baking powder, salt and basil.

3. In another bowl combine milk and eggs; blend well. Add to flour mixture; stir just until moist. Add peppers.

4. Spoon batter into prepared muffin tin, dividing evenly. Bake in preheated oven for 15 minutes or until golden brown.

ham, pepper and onion muffins

1/4 cup	butter *or* margarine	50 mL
3/4 cup	finely chopped onions	175 mL
3/4 cup	finely chopped ham	175 mL
2 cups	all-purpose flour	500 mL
2 tbsp	granulated sugar	25 mL
1 tbsp	baking powder	15 mL
1 tsp	coarsely ground black pepper	5 mL
1/2 tsp	salt	2 mL
1 cup	milk	250 mL
1	large egg	1

Preheat oven to 400° F (200° C)
Muffin tin, greased or paper-lined

1. In a frying pan heat butter over medium-high heat. Add onions; cook for about 2 minutes. Set aside.

2. In a bowl combine ham, flour, sugar, baking powder, pepper and salt; blend well.

3. In another bowl combine milk, egg and onions. Add to flour mixture; stir just until moist.

4. Spoon batter into prepared muffin tin, dividing evenly. Bake in preheated oven for 20 to 25 minutes.

turkey ham, cheese and pepper muffins

1/4 cup	butter *or* margarine	50 mL
1/2 cup	minced sweet onions	125 mL
1/4 cup	minced green bell peppers	50 mL
1	garlic clove, minced or pressed	1
2 cups	all-purpose flour	500 mL
1 tbsp	baking powder	15 mL
1 tsp	salt	5 mL
1/2 tsp	pepper	2 mL
1 cup	milk	250 mL
2	eggs	2
1 cup	finely diced turkey ham	250 mL
1/2 cup	diced Cheddar cheese	125 mL
1/4 cup	shelled roasted sunflower seeds	50 mL

Preheat oven to 375° F (190° C)
Muffin tin, well-greased

1. In a skillet heat butter over medium-high heat. Add onions, green peppers and garlic. Cook, stirring, for 5 to 7 minutes or until onions are translucent.

2. In a bowl combine flour, baking powder, salt and pepper.

3. In another bowl combine milk and eggs; beat well. Add to flour mixture; mix well. Add vegetables with drippings, turkey and cheese; stir just until moist.

4. Spoon batter into prepared muffin tin, dividing evenly. Sprinkle with sunflower seeds. Bake in preheated oven for 25 to 30 minutes.

onion-parsley muffins

2 cups	all-purpose flour	500 mL
1 tbsp	granulated sugar	15 mL
3 tsp	baking powder	15 mL
1 1/2 tsp	salt	7 mL
1/4 cup	vegetable oil	50 mL
1 cup	milk	250 mL
4	green onions, chopped	4
1/4 cup	chopped parsley	50 mL

Preheat oven to 400° F (200° C)
Muffin tin, greased

1. In a bowl sift together flour, sugar, baking powder and salt.

2. In another bowl combine oil, milk, green onions and parsley. Add to dry ingredients; mix just until well-blended.

3. Spoon batter into prepared muffin tin, filling three-quarters full. Bake in preheated oven for 20 to 25 minutes or until toothpick inserted in center comes out clean.

chili-pepper corn muffins

1 cup	all-purpose flour	250 mL
1 cup	yellow cornmeal	250 mL
1 tbsp	baking powder	15 mL
1 1/2 tsp	ground cumin	7 mL
1 tsp	crushed red bell pepper	5 mL
1/2 tsp	salt	2 mL
2/3 cup	sour cream	150 mL
2/3 cup	milk	150 mL
2 tbsp	butter or margarine, melted	25 mL
1	large egg	1
1 3/4 cups	finely shredded sharp Cheddar cheese	425 mL
1/3 cup	finely diced seeded hot chili peppers or jalapeño peppers	75 mL
1/3 cup	finely chopped green onions	75 mL
1/3 cup	canned whole kernel corn, drained	75 mL

Preheat oven to 375° F (190° C)
12-cup muffin tin, greased or paper-lined

1. In a bowl combine flour, cornmeal, baking powder, cumin, red pepper and salt.

2. In another bowl combine sour cream, milk, butter and egg; whisk until blended. Add cornmeal mixture; mix well. Add cheese, chili peppers, green onions and corn; blend well.

3. Spoon batter into prepared muffin tin, filling to top. Bake in preheated oven for 25 to 30 minutes or until toothpick inserted in center comes out clean.

easy orange cornmeal muffins

1 cup	yellow cornmeal	250 mL
1 cup	all-purpose flour	250 mL
1/3 cup	granulated sugar	75 mL
4 tsp	baking powder	20 mL
1/4 tsp	salt	1 mL
1	egg, slightly beaten	1
1 cup	milk	250 mL
1/4 cup	vegetable oil	50 mL
1 tbsp	grated orange or lemon zest	15 mL

Preheat oven to 425° F (220° C)
Muffin tin, greased

1. In a bowl combine cornmeal, flour, sugar, baking powder and salt.

2. In another bowl combine egg, milk, oil and orange zest. Add to cornmeal mixture; stir just until blended.

3. Spoon batter into prepared muffin tin, filling three-quarters full. Bake in preheated oven for about 15 minutes or until lightly browned.

cornmeal sausage gems

8 oz	bulk beef or pork sausage, formed into 12 small patties	250 g
1 cup	all-purpose flour	250 mL
1 cup	cornmeal	250 mL
2 tsp	baking powder	10 mL
1/2 tsp	salt	2 mL
1 tbsp	granulated sugar	15 mL
1	egg	1
1 cup	milk	250 mL
2 tbsp	sausage drippings	25 mL

Preheat oven to 425° F (220° C)
12-cup muffin tin, greased

1. In a frying pan over medium-high heat, brown patties. Pour off drippings, saving as they accumulate.

2. In a bowl sift together flour, cornmeal, baking powder, salt and sugar.

3. In another bowl beat egg. Add milk and sausage drippings; mix well. Add to flour mixture; stir just until flour is dampened.

4. Place 1 patty in bottom of each muffin cup. Top with batter. Bake in preheated oven for 20 minutes.

sunny corn muffins

1 1/4 cups	yellow cornmeal	300 mL
3/4 cup	sunflower seed	175 mL
1/2 cup	all-purpose flour	125 mL
2 tbsp	granulated sugar	25 mL
2 tsp	baking powder	10 mL
3/4 tsp	salt	4 mL
1 cup	milk	250 mL
1	egg	1
3 tbsp	oil	45 mL

Preheat oven to 425° F (220° C)
12-cup muffin tin, greased

1. In a bowl combine cornmeal, sunflower seed, flour, sugar, baking powder and salt.

2. In another bowl combine milk, egg and oil. Add to dry ingredients; stir to combine well (batter will be thin.)

3. Spoon batter into prepared muffin tin, dividing evenly. Bake in preheated oven for 25 minutes.

golden squash muffins

2 1/4 cups	all-purpose flour	550 mL
1/3 cup	granulated sugar	75 mL
2 1/2 tsp	baking powder	12 mL
1/4 tsp	salt	1 mL
1/3 cup	softened butter or margarine	75 mL
1	egg	1
3/4 cup	mashed cooked winter squash	175 mL
1 tsp	grated orange zest	5 mL
1 cup	milk	250 mL
1/4 cup	golden raisins	50 mL

Preheat oven to 400° F (200° C)
12-cup muffin tin, greased or lined with foil cups

1. In a bowl combine flour, sugar, baking powder and salt. With a pastry blender or 2 knives, cut in butter until mixture is crumbly.

2. In another bowl beat egg. Add squash, orange zest and milk; blend well. Add to flour mixture; stir just until blended. Fold in raisins.

3. Spoon batter into prepared muffin tin, filling three-quarters full. Bake in preheated oven for 20 to 25 minutes.

best zucchini muffins

1 cup	all-purpose flour	250 mL
1 cup	whole wheat flour	250 mL
1 1/2 tsp	baking powder	7 mL
1/2 tsp	baking soda	2 mL
1 tsp	cinnamon	5 mL
1/2 tsp	allspice	2 mL
1 tsp	salt	5 mL
1	egg	1
1/4 cup	vegetable oil	50 mL
1/2 cup	granulated sugar	125 mL
1 cup	grated zucchini	250 mL
1/2 cup	milk	125 mL

Preheat oven to 400° F (200° C)
12-cup muffin tin, greased

1. In a bowl combine all-purpose flour, whole wheat flour, baking powder, baking soda, cinnamon, allspice and salt. Make a well in the center.

2. In another bowl beat egg. Add oil, sugar, zucchini and milk; blend well. Add to dry ingredients; stir just until moist (batter will be lumpy.)

3. Spoon batter into prepared muffin tin, filling three-quarters full. Bake in preheated oven for 20 to 25 minutes.

ORANGE UPSIDE-DOWN CRANBERRY MUFFINS (PAGE 171) ➤

chocolate zucchini muffins

1 cup	all-purpose flour	250 mL
1/2 cup	whole wheat flour	125 mL
1/3 cup	quick-cooking rolled oats	75 mL
1 tsp	baking soda	5 mL
1/2 cup	softened butter	125 mL
1/2 cup	granulated sugar	125 mL
2	eggs	2
2 tbsp	sour cream *or* plain yogurt	25 mL
1 tsp	vanilla	5 mL
1/2 tsp	grated lemon zest	2 mL
2 cups	packed grated zucchini	500 mL
4 oz	grated bittersweet chocolate	125 g
1/2 cup	chopped pecans (optional)	125 mL

Preheat oven to 400° F (200° C)
Muffin tin, greased

1. In a bowl combine all-purpose flour, whole wheat flour, oats and baking soda.

2. In another bowl combine butter and sugar; cream until fluffy. Add eggs, sour cream, vanilla and lemon zest; beat well. Add flour mixture alternately with zucchini; blend well. Add chocolate and pecans; beat well.

3. Spoon batter into prepared muffin tin, filling three-quarters full. Bake in preheated oven for about 20 minutes or until toothpick inserted in center comes out clean and dry.

< APPLE STREUSEL PUMPKIN MUFFINS (PAGE 177)

lemon zucchini muffins

2 cups	all-purpose flour	500 mL
2 tsp	baking powder	10 mL
1/2 tsp	baking soda	2 mL
1/2 tsp	salt	2 mL
1/8 tsp	freshly grated nutmeg	.5 mL
3/4 cup	granulated sugar	175 mL
1	egg	1
1/2 cup	milk	125 mL
1/2 cup	vegetable oil	125 mL
2 tbsp	freshly squeezed lemon juice	25 mL
1 cup	grated unpeeled zucchini, squeezed dry	250 mL
	Grated zest of 1 lemon	

Preheat oven to 400° F (200° C)
Muffin tin, greased

1. In a bowl combine flour, baking powder, baking soda, salt, nutmeg and sugar; stir with a fork until well blended.

2. In another bowl beat together egg, milk, oil and lemon juice. Add to flour mixture; blend well. Add zucchini and lemon zest; stir with a fork just until blended (batter will be thick.)

3. Spoon batter into prepared muffin tin, filling three-quarters full. Bake in preheated oven for 20 to 25 minutes.

zucchini nut muffins

4	eggs	4
1 cup	granulated sugar	250 mL
1/2 tsp	vanilla	2 mL
1 cup	vegetable oil	250 mL
2 cups	grated unpeeled zucchini	500 mL
3 cups	all-purpose flour	750 mL
1 1/2 tsp	baking powder	7 mL
1 tsp	baking soda	5 mL
1 tsp	salt	5 mL
1 tsp	cinnamon	5 mL
1 cup	chopped walnuts	250 mL

Preheat oven to 375° F (190° C)
Muffin tin, greased or paper-lined

1. In a bowl combine eggs, sugar and vanilla; beat for 2 minutes. Slowly add oil; beat for 2 minutes. Add zucchini.

2. In another bowl combine flour, baking powder, baking soda, salt and cinnamon. Add walnuts; blend well. Add zucchini mixture; stir just until blended.

3. Spoon batter into prepared muffin tin, filling three-quarters full. Bake in preheated oven for 25 to 30 minutes.

spiced zucchini muffins

1 cup	all-purpose flour	250 mL
1 cup	whole wheat flour	250 mL
1 1/2 tsp	baking powder	7 mL
1/2 tsp	baking soda	2 mL
1 tsp	cinnamon	5 mL
1/2 tsp	allspice	2 mL
1 tsp	salt	5 mL
1	egg	1
1/4 cup	oil	50 mL
1/2 cup	granulated sugar	125 mL
1 cup	grated zucchini	250 mL
1/2 cup	milk	125 mL

Preheat oven to 400° F (200° C)

12-cup muffin tin, greased

1. In a bowl combine all-purpose flour, whole wheat flour, baking powder, baking soda, cinnamon, allspice and salt. Make a well in the center.

2. In another bowl beat egg. Add oil, sugar, zucchini and milk; blend well. Add to dry ingredients; stir just until blended (batter will be lumpy).

3. Spoon batter into prepared muffin tin, filling three-quarters full. Bake in preheated oven for 20 to 25 minutes.

whole wheat zucchini muffins

1 cup	whole wheat flour	250 mL
1/2 tsp	baking powder	2 mL
1/2 tsp	baking soda	2 mL
1 tsp	cinnamon	5 mL
1/3 cup	chopped nuts	75 mL
1	egg	1
1/2 cup	granulated sugar	125 mL
1/2 cup	oil	125 mL
1 tsp	vanilla	5 mL
1 cup	grated zucchini	250 mL

Preheat oven to 400° F (200° C)

12-cup muffin tin, greased or paper-lined

1. In a bowl combine flour, baking powder, baking soda, cinnamon and nuts. Make a well in the center.

2. In another bowl combine egg, sugar, oil, vanilla and zucchini. Add to dry ingredients; mix just until blended.

3. Spoon batter into prepared muffin tin, filling three-quarters full. Bake in preheated oven for 20 to 25 minutes or until toothpick inserted in center comes out clean and dry.

holiday muffins

christmas morning muffins

2 cups	all-purpose flour	500 mL
1/2 cup	wheat germ	125 mL
4 tsp	baking powder	20 mL
1 tsp	baking soda	5 mL
1 tsp	salt	5 mL
1/2 cup	granulated sugar	125 mL
1 tsp	ground cardamom	5 mL
1/2 cup	chopped almonds	125 mL
1/2 cup	raisins	125 mL
1 cup	glazed mixed fruit	250 mL
2	eggs	2
1 cup	buttermilk	250 mL
1/2 cup	melted butter or margarine	125 mL

Preheat oven to 375° F (190° C)
18-cup muffin tin, greased or paper-lined

1. In a bowl combine flour, wheat germ, baking powder, baking soda, salt, sugar, cardamom, almonds, raisins and mixed fruit.

2. In another bowl whisk together eggs, buttermilk and butter. Add to dry ingredients; stir quickly just until ingredients are moist.

3. Spoon batter into prepared muffin tin, dividing evenly. Bake in preheated oven for 20 to 25 minutes.

christmas tea muffins

2 cups	all-purpose flour	500 mL
1 tbsp	baking powder	15 mL
1/2 cup	granulated sugar	125 mL
1 tsp	salt	5 mL
3/4 cup	milk	175 mL
3 tbsp	maraschino cherry juice	45 mL
1/4 cup	oil	50 mL
1	egg	1
1/3 cup	chopped maraschino cherries	75 mL
1/4 cup	chopped almonds	50 mL

Preheat oven to 375° F (190° C)
12-cup muffin tin, greased or paper-lined

1. In a bowl sift together flour, baking powder, sugar and salt.

2. In another bowl whisk together milk, cherry juice, oil and egg. Add to dry ingredients; cherries and almonds. Stir just until blended.

3. Spoon batter into prepared muffin tin, dividing evenly. Bake in preheated oven for 25 minutes.

traditional cranberry muffins

1 1/2 cups	all-purpose flour	375 mL
1/2 cup	granulated sugar	125 mL
1 tbsp	baking powder	15 mL
1/4 tsp	salt	1 mL
1	egg	1
1 cup	milk	250 mL
1/3 cup	melted butter or margarine	75 mL
1 cup	fresh cranberries *or* frozen cranberries, thawed and drained	250 mL
1/2 cup	chopped nuts	125 mL

Preheat oven to 375° F (190° C)
12-cup muffin tin, greased

1. In a bowl combine flour, sugar, baking powder and salt.

2. In another bowl whisk together egg, milk and butter. Add to dry ingredients; stir just until moist and blended. Fold in cranberries and nuts.

3. Spoon batter into prepared muffin tin, dividing evenly. Bake in preheated oven for 20 to 25 minutes.

cranberry-filled almond muffins

1 1/2 cups	all-purpose flour	375 mL
1/2 cup	granulated sugar	125 mL
1 tsp	baking powder	5 mL
1/4 tsp	baking soda	1 mL
1/4 tsp	salt	1 mL
2	eggs	2
1/4 cup	melted margarine	50 mL
1/2 cup	sour cream	125 mL
1/2 tsp	almond extract	2 mL
1/2 cup	sliced almonds	125 mL
FILLING		
1/2 cup	whole berry cranberry sauce	125 mL
1/4 cup	sliced almonds	50 mL

Preheat oven to 375° F (190° C)
Muffin tin, greased or paper-lined

1. In a bowl combine flour, sugar, baking powder, baking soda and salt.

2. In another bowl whisk together eggs, margarine, sour cream and almond extract; blend well. Add almonds. Add to flour mixture; stir just until blended.

3. Spoon batter into prepared muffin tin, filling half full. Add 1 tbsp (15 mL) cranberry sauce to each; top with remaining batter. Sprinkle evenly with almonds. Bake in preheated oven for 30 to 35 minutes or until golden brown.

cranberry applesauce muffins

Preheat oven to 400° F (200° C)
12-cup muffin tin, greased

1 3/4 cups	all-purpose flour	425 mL
1/4 cup	granulated sugar	50 mL
1 1/2 tsp	baking powder	7 mL
1/2 tsp	baking soda	2 mL
1/2 tsp	salt	2 mL
1	egg	1
3/4 cup	milk	175 mL
3/4 cup	sweetened applesauce	175 mL
1/4 cup	melted butter or margarine	50 mL
1 cup	coarsely chopped cranberries	250 mL
2 tbsp	all-purpose flour	25 mL
TOPPING		
1/4 cup	granulated sugar	50 mL
1/2 tsp	cinnamon	2 mL

1. In a bowl combine flour, sugar, baking powder, baking soda and salt. Make a well in the center.

2. In another bowl combine egg, milk, applesauce and butter; mix well. Add to flour mixture; stir quickly just until batter is moist.

3. In another bowl combine cranberries and flour; toss well. Fold into batter.

4. Spoon batter into prepared muffin tin, filling three-quarters full. Sprinkle tops with sugar and cinnamon. Bake in preheated oven for 20 to 25 minutes.

apricot cranberry bran muffins

Preheat oven to 400° F (200° C)
12-cup muffin tin, greased or paper-lined

1 3/4 cups	all-purpose flour	425 mL
1/3 cup	packed brown sugar	75 mL
2 tsp	baking powder	10 mL
1/2 tsp	salt	2 mL
2	eggs	2
2/3 cup	orange juice	150 mL
2 tsp	grated orange zest	10 mL
1/4 cup	vegetable oil	50 mL
1 cup	all-bran cereal	250 mL
2/3 cup	chopped dried apricots	150 mL
3/4 cup	whole berry cranberry sauce	175 mL

1. In a bowl combine flour, brown sugar, baking powder and salt. Make a well in the center.

2. In another bowl whisk together eggs, orange juice, orange zest and oil. Add cereal and apricots; blend well. Add to flour mixture; stir just until blended. Fold in cranberry sauce.

3. Spoon batter into prepared muffin tin, dividing evenly. Bake in preheated oven for 25 to 30 minutes or until golden brown.

cranberry banana breakfast muffins

2 cups	uncooked oat bran hot cereal	500 mL
1/2 cup	firmly packed brown sugar	125 mL
1/4 cup	all-purpose flour	50 mL
2 tsp	baking powder	10 mL
1/2 tsp	salt	2 mL
1/2 tsp	cinnamon	2 mL
1/2 cup	finely chopped cranberries	125 mL
2/3 cup	cranberry juice	150 mL
1/2 cup	ripe mashed bananas	125 mL
2	egg whites, slightly beaten	2
3 tbsp	vegetable oil	45 mL

Preheat oven to 400° F (200° C)
12-cup muffin tin, greased or paper-lined

1. In a bowl combine oat bran, brown sugar, flour, baking powder, salt and cinnamon. Add cranberries; stir gently.

2. In another bowl combine cranberry juice, bananas, egg whites and oil. Add to dry ingredients; mix just until moist and blended.

3. Spoon batter into prepared muffin tin, filling to top. Bake in preheated oven for 20 to 25 minutes or until golden brown.

cranberry honey muffins

1/3 cup	softened margarine	75 mL
1/3 cup	honey	75 mL
1	egg, well-beaten	1
1 1/4 cups	chopped cranberries *or* thick cranberry sauce	300 mL
	Grated zest of 1 orange	
2/3 cup	milk	150 mL
2 cups	all-purpose flour	500 mL
1 tbsp	baking powder	15 mL
1 tsp	salt	5 mL

Preheat oven to 400° F (200° C)
Muffin tin, greased or paper-lined

1. In a bowl cream together margarine and honey. Add egg, cranberries, orange zest and milk; mix well.

2. In another bowl combine flour, baking powder and salt. Add to cranberry mixture; stir just until ingredients are moist.

3. Spoon batter into prepared muffin tin, filling three-quarters full. Bake in preheated oven for about 20 minutes.

cranberry fruitcake muffins

2/3 cup	all-purpose flour	150 mL
2/3 cup	whole wheat flour	150 mL
1/2 cup	rolled oats	125 mL
1 1/2 tsp	baking soda	7 mL
1 tsp	ginger	5 mL
2	eggs	2
1/2 cup	honey	125 mL
1/3 cup	orange juice	75 mL
1/4 cup	oil	50 mL
1 tsp	vanilla	5 mL
1 cup	cranberries	250 mL
3/4 cup	shredded apples	175 mL

Preheat oven to 400° F (200° C)
Muffin tin, greased or paper-lined

1. In a bowl combine all-purpose flour, whole wheat flour, oats, baking soda and ginger.

2. In another bowl whisk together eggs, honey, orange juice, oil and vanilla. Add cranberries and apples; stir well. Add to flour mixture; stir just until blended.

3. Spoon batter into prepared muffin tin, filling three-quarters full. Bake in preheated oven for 15 to 20 minutes.

cranberry nut muffins

2 cups	all-purpose flour	500 mL
3/4 cup	granulated sugar	175 mL
1/2 cup	chopped nuts	125 mL
1 tsp	baking powder	5 mL
1 tsp	baking soda	5 mL
2 tsp	grated orange zest	10 mL
3/4 cup	mayonnaise	175 mL
1/4 cup	frozen undiluted orange juice concentrate, thawed	50 mL
2	eggs, beaten	2
2 cups	fresh or frozen whole cranberries	500 mL

Preheat oven to 350° F (180° C)
12-cup muffin tin, greased

1. In a bowl combine flour, sugar, nuts, baking powder, baking soda and orange zest.

2. In another bowl combine mayonnaise, orange juice, eggs and cranberries; mix well. Add to flour mixture; stir just until blended.

3. Spoon batter into prepared muffin tin, filling to top. Bake in preheated oven for 20 to 25 minutes.

orange upside-down cranberry muffin

Preheat oven to 375° F (190° C)
15-cup muffin tin, sprayed with vegetable spray

	Frozen orange juice concentrate	
	Granulated sugar	
2 1/2 cups	all-purpose flour	625 mL
1/3 cup	granulated sugar	75 mL
1 tsp	salt	5 mL
1 tbsp	baking powder	15 mL
1 tsp	baking soda	5 mL
1 cup	chopped pecans	250 mL
	Grated zest of 2 oranges	
1 cup	whole berry cranberry sauce	250 mL
2/3 cup	orange juice	150 mL
1 tbsp	lemon juice	15 mL
2	eggs	2
1/4 cup	oil	50 mL

1. Into each prepared muffin cup spoon 1 tsp (5 mL) frozen concentrate and 1/2 tsp (2 mL) sugar. Set aside.

2. In a bowl combine flour, sugar, salt, baking powder, baking soda, pecans and orange zest. Make a well in the center.

3. In another bowl whisk together cranberry sauce, orange juice, lemon juice, eggs and oil. Add to flour mixture; stir quickly just until blended.

4. Spoon batter into muffin tin, dividing evenly. Bake in preheated oven for 25 to 30 minutes or until browned. Remove from oven; let stand for 5 minutes. Turn pans upside-down so orange mixture is on top. Spoon any remaining sauce over muffins.

stuffed orange cranberry muffins

Preheat oven to 375° F (190° C)
12-cup muffin tin, paper-lined

1	large orange, seeds removed and quartered	1
3/4 cup	boiling water	175 mL
1/4 cup	oil	50 mL
1	egg	1
2 cups	all-purpose flour	500 mL
2 tsp	baking powder	10 mL
1 tsp	baking soda	5 mL
1/2 tsp	salt	2 mL
3/4 cup + 2 tbsp	lightly packed brown sugar	175 mL + 25 mL
3/4 cup	cranberries	175 mL
4 oz	cream cheese, cut into 12 pieces	125 g

1. In a blender combine orange pieces and boiling water; blend until almost smooth. Add oil and egg; blend well.

2. In a bowl combine flour, baking powder, baking soda, salt, brown sugar and cranberries. Add orange mixture; stir quickly just until moist.

3. Spoon batter into prepared muffin tin, filling half full. Add 1 cream cheese piece; top with remaining batter. Bake in preheated oven for 20 to 25 minutes or until lightly browned.

cranberry streusel muffins

Preheat oven to 375° F (190° C)
Muffin tin, greased or paper-lined

STREUSEL TOPPING

2 tbsp	all-purpose flour	25 mL
2 tbsp	granulated sugar	25 mL
1/4 tsp	cinnamon	1 mL
2 tbsp	butter *or* margarine	25 mL
1/4 cup	softened butter or margarine	50 mL
1/4 cup	granulated sugar	50 mL
1	egg	1
1 tsp	vanilla	5 mL
2 cups	all-purpose flour	500 mL
2 tsp	baking powder	10 mL
Pinch	salt	Pinch
1/2 cup	milk	125 mL
2 cups	coarsely chopped cranberries	500 mL
1/2 cup	icing sugar	125 mL

1. In a bowl combine flour, sugar and cinnamon. Cut in butter until mixture is crumbly. Set aside.

2. In another bowl combine butter and sugar; cream until light and fluffy. Beat in egg and vanilla.

3. In a bowl combine flour, baking powder and salt. Add to creamed mixture alternately with milk; stir just until moist. In another bowl combine cranberries and icing sugar; fold into batter.

4. Spoon batter into prepared muffin tin, filling two-thirds full. Sprinkle with streusel topping. Bake in preheated oven for 25 to 30 minutes.

cranberry swirl muffins

Preheat oven to 400° F (200° C)
12-cup muffin tin, paper-lined

1/4 cup	shortening	50 mL
1/2 cup	granulated sugar	125 mL
2	egg whites	2
1 1/2 cups	all-purpose flour	375 mL
2 tsp	baking powder	10 mL
1/2 tsp	salt (optional)	2 mL
3/4 cup	milk	175 mL
1/2 cup	cranberry sauce	125 mL

1. In a bowl cream together shortening and sugar. Add egg whites; beat until fairly smooth. Add flour, baking powder, salt and milk; stir just until blended. Add cranberry sauce; swirl with spatula through batter.

2. Spoon batter into prepared muffin tin, dividing evenly. Bake in preheated oven for 20 minutes or until golden brown.

cranberry tea muffins

2 cups	cake flour	500 mL
1/3 cup	granulated sugar	75 mL
2 tsp	baking powder	10 mL
1/2 tsp	salt	2 mL
2	eggs	2
3/4 cup	milk	175 mL
1/4 cup	melted butter	50 mL
1 cup	freshly chopped whole cranberries	250 mL
1 tsp	grated orange zest	5 mL

Preheat oven to 400° F (200° C)
18-cup muffin tin, greased or paper-lined

1. In a bowl combine flour, sugar, baking powder and salt.

2. In another bowl whisk together eggs, milk and butter. Add to flour mixture; stir quickly just until blended. Fold in cranberries and orange zest.

3. Spoon batter into prepared muffin tin, dividing evenly. Bake in preheated oven for 20 to 25 minutes.

holiday gingerbread muffins

1 1/2 cups	all-purpose flour	375 mL
1 1/2 cups	whole wheat flour	375 mL
1/3 cup	firmly packed brown sugar	75 mL
3 1/2 tsp	baking powder	17 mL
2 tsp	ginger	10 mL
3/4 tsp	cinnamon	4 mL
1/2 tsp	salt	2 mL
1	egg	1
1 1/4 cups	milk	300 mL
1/2 cup	molasses	125 mL
1/2 cup	melted margarine	125 mL

Preheat oven to 400° F (200° C)
12-cup muffin tin, greased or paper-lined

1. In a bowl combine all-purpose flour, whole wheat flour, brown sugar, baking powder, ginger, cinnamon and salt. Make a well in the center.

2. In another bowl whisk together egg, milk, molasses and margarine. Add to dry ingredients; stir just until moist.

3. Spoon batter into prepared muffin tin, filling to top. Bake in preheated oven for about 20 minutes.

mincemeat bran muffins

Preheat oven to 375° F (190° C)
2 12-cup muffin tins, greased

2 1/4 cups	all-purpose flour	550 mL
1 1/4 cups	natural bran	300 mL
2 tsp	baking powder	10 mL
2 tsp	baking soda	10 mL
1 tsp	salt	5 mL
2	eggs, beaten	2
3/4 cup	vegetable oil	175 mL
3/4 cup	granulated sugar	175 mL
1/4 cup	molasses *or* brown sugar	50 mL
2 cups	milk	500 mL
1 1/2 cups	mincemeat	375 mL

1. In a bowl combine flour, bran, baking powder, baking soda and salt. Make a well in the center.

2. In another bowl beat together eggs, oil and sugar. Add molasses, milk and mincemeat; beat well. Add to dry ingredients; stir just until moist.

3. Spoon batter into prepared muffin tins, filling three-quarters full. Bake in preheated oven for 18 to 20 minutes.

snow muffins

Preheat oven to 375° F (190° C)
12-cup muffin tin, greased

2 cups	all-purpose flour	500 mL
1 cup	lightly packed brown sugar	250 mL
1 tbsp	baking powder	15 mL
1 tsp	salt	5 mL
3 tbsp	margarine, melted	45 mL
1 cup	milk	250 mL
1 1/2 cups	snow	375 mL
3/4 cup	raisins *or* currants	175 mL

1. In a bowl combine flour, brown sugar, baking powder and salt; mix well. Add margarine and milk; mixture will be lumpy. Quickly add snow and raisins; stir just until blended.

2. Spoon batter into prepared muffin tin, dividing evenly. Bake in preheated oven for 20 to 25 minutes or until lightly browned.

muffin stuff

At first, when I was given this recipe, I thought it was an April fool's joke! Before making muffins collect fresh, loosely-packed snow.

passover apple muffins

FILLING

1/3 cup	granulated sugar	75 mL
1 1/2 tsp	cinnamon	7 mL
1 tbsp	margarine, melted	15 mL
4	egg yolks	4
2/3 cup	granulated sugar	150 mL
2 cups	grated apples	500 mL
1/2 tsp	grated lemon zest	2 mL
1 tbsp	lemon juice	15 mL
1 cup	matzo meal	250 mL
1/2 tsp	cinnamon	2 mL
4	egg whites, stiffly beaten	4
Pinch	salt	Pinch

Preheat oven to 425° F (220° C)
Muffin tin, greased

1. In a bowl combine sugar, cinnamon and margarine; mix well. Set aside.

2. In another bowl beat together egg yolks and sugar. Add apples, lemon zest, lemon juice, matzo meal and cinnamon; mix well. Fold in egg whites and salt.

3. Spoon batter into prepared muffin tin, filling half full. Sprinkle with filling. Top with remaining batter. Bake in preheated oven for 15 to 20 minutes.

passover blueberry muffins

1 cup	granulated sugar	250 mL
1/2 cup	oil	125 mL
3	eggs	3
1/2 cup	cake meal	125 mL
1/4 cup	potato starch	50 mL
1/4 tsp	salt	1 mL
1	pkg (10 oz [300 g]) frozen blueberries, thawed and drained	1
	Cinnamon (optional)	
	Granulated sugar (optional)	

Preheat oven to 350° F (180° C)
Muffin tin, greased or paper-lined

1. In a bowl combine sugar, oil and eggs; beat well.

2. In another bowl sift together cake meal, potato starch and salt. Add to egg mixture; stir until blended. Fold in blueberries.

3. Spoon batter into prepared muffin tin, filling to top. Sprinkle with cinnamon and sugar. Bake in preheated oven for 30 minutes or until browned.

passover cocoa brownies

1/2 cup	cocoa powder	125 mL
1/2 cup	boiling water	125 mL
2	eggs	2
1 cup	granulated sugar	250 mL
1/2 cup	oil	125 mL
1/2 cup	cake meal	125 mL
1 tsp	instant coffee, dissolved in 2 tsp. (10 mL) water	5 mL
1/2 cup	chopped walnuts	125 mL

Preheat oven to 400° F (200° C)
Muffin tin, greased

1. In a bowl combine cocoa and water; mix to form a paste. Set aside.

2. In a bowl combine eggs, sugar and oil; beat until well blended. Add cocoa paste; mix well. Add cake meal, coffee mixture and walnuts.

3. Spoon batter into prepared muffin tin, dividing evenly. Bake in preheated oven for 20 to 25 minutes.

passover popovers

1/2 cup	oil *or* shortening	125 mL
1 1/2 cups	water	375 mL
2 tbsp	granulated sugar	25 mL
1 1/2 cups	cake meal	375 mL
7	eggs	7

Preheat oven to 450° F (230° C)
Muffin tin, greased

1. In a saucepan over medium-high heat, combine oil, water and sugar; bring to a boil. Remove from heat. Add cake meal; cool slightly. Add eggs one at a time; beat after each addition.

2. In preheated oven heat prepared muffin tin. Spoon batter into cups, filling three-quarters full. Bake in preheated oven for 20 minutes. Lower heat to 350° F (180° C); bake for another 25 to 30 minutes.

mashed potato muffins

10	medium-sized potatoes	10
1 tsp	salt	5 mL
1/2 tsp	pepper	2 mL
2 tbsp	oil	25 mL
4	eggs, beaten	4
2	onions, chopped	2

Preheat oven to 400° F (200° C)
2 12-cup muffin tins, greased

1. In a saucepan of boiling water, cook potatoes until soft. In a bowl combine cooked potatoes, salt, pepper and oil; mash until smooth. Add eggs; mix well.

2. In a frying pan over medium-high heat, cook onions for about 2 minutes. Add to potato mixture; stir well.

3. In prehcated oven heat prepared muffin tins. Spoon batter into cups. Bake in preheated oven for 30 to 40 minutes.

apple streusel pumpkin muffins

STREUSEL TOPPING

2 tbsp	all-purpose flour	25 mL
1/4 cup	granulated sugar	50 mL
1/2 tsp	cinnamon	2 mL
4 tsp	butter	20 mL

2 1/2 cups	all-purpose flour	625 mL
2 cups	granulated sugar	500 mL
1 tsp	baking soda	5 mL
1 tbsp	pumpkin pie spice	15 mL
1/2 tsp	salt	2 mL
2	eggs, beaten	2
1 cup	canned pumpkin	250 mL
1/2 cup	vegetable oil	125 mL
2 cups	finely chopped apples	500 mL

Preheat oven to 375° F (190° C)
Muffin tin, greased or paper-lined

1. In a bowl combine flour, sugar and cinnamon. Cut in butter; mix until coarse and crumbly. Set aside.

2. In another bowl combine flour, sugar, baking soda, pumpkin pie spice and salt. Make a well in the center.

3. In another bowl combine eggs, pumpkin and oil; stir just until blended. Add apples; blend well. Add to dry ingredients; stir just until moist.

4. Spoon batter into prepared muffin tin, filling three-quarters full. Sprinkle with topping. Bake in preheated oven for 25 to 30 minutes.

traditional pumpkin muffins

1 cup	all-purpose flour	250 mL
1 cup	whole wheat flour	250 mL
1/2 cup	lightly packed brown sugar	125 mL
1 tbsp	baking powder	15 mL
1 1/2 tsp	cinnamon	7 mL
1/2 tsp	nutmeg	2 mL
2	egg whites	2
1/2 cup	milk	125 mL
1 cup	canned pumpkin	250 mL
1/4 cup	oil	50 mL
1/2 tsp	vanilla	2 mL
3/4 cup	raisins	175 mL

Preheat oven to 400° F (200° C)

12-cup muffin tin, greased or paper-lined

1. In a bowl combine all-purpose flour, whole wheat flour, brown sugar, baking powder, cinnamon and nutmeg; blend well. Make a well in the center.

2. In another bowl beat egg whites. Add milk, pumpkin, oil and vanilla; blend well. Add to dry ingredients; stir just until moist. Add raisins.

3. Spoon batter into prepared muffin tin, filling three-quarters full. Bake in preheated oven for 20 to 25 minutes or until browned.

orange pumpkin muffins

1 3/4 cups	all-purpose flour	425 mL
2 1/2 tsp	baking powder	12 mL
1/2 tsp	baking soda	2 mL
1/2 tsp	salt	2 mL
2/3 cup	brown sugar	150 mL
1 tsp	cinnamon	5 mL
1/4 tsp	nutmeg	1 mL
Pinch	ginger	Pinch
Pinch	mace	Pinch
1	egg	1
1/4 cup	melted butter or margarine, cooled	50 mL
1/2 cup	milk	125 mL
	Finely grated zest of 1 orange	
1/2 cup	orange juice	125 mL
3/4 cup	canned pumpkin purée	175 mL

Preheat oven to 400° F (200° C)

12-cup muffin tin, greased or paper-lined

1. In a bowl combine flour, baking powder, baking soda, salt, brown sugar, cinnamon, nutmeg, ginger and mace. Make a well in the center.

2. In another bowl whisk together egg, butter, milk, orange zest, orange juice and pumpkin. Add to dry ingredients; stir just until blended.

3. Spoon batter into prepared muffin tin, filling three-quarters full. Bake in preheated oven for about 20 minutes.

index

a

b